Magic Guidebooks

Universal Studios

HOLLYWOOD

2024

FAST AND INFORMATIVE VACATION PLANNING!

Insider Secrets, Dining Reviews, & Tips
for Universal Studios Hollywood,
The Wizarding World of Harry Potter,
Super Nintendo World, CityWalk, & More!

ISBN: 979-8-9889768-2-0

Magic Guidebooks

Universal Studios Hollywood 2024

- Fast and useful insider tips and recommendations
- Honest ride and dining reviews with recommendations
- A FULL guide Super Nintendo World and how to best experience attractions like Mario Kart, interactive elements, Toadstool Cafe and more!
- Dedicated Super Nintendo World chapter with the best tips for experiencing the land!
- The Wizarding World of Harry Potter in detail! Learn the top tips for a magical visit to Hogsmeade Village
- Money and time-saving tactics for worry-free planning
- Hotel reviews near Universal Studios Hollywood and other attractions in Los Angeles

Table of Contents

INTRODUCTION

ABOUT THIS GUIDE

When developing and writing this book, we had *you* in mind. Maybe you're a first-time visitor to Universal Studios Hollywood, or perhaps you've frequented it over the years. Wherever you come from and whatever your experience, we wanted to provide a complete guide from start to finish, while also giving a critique of the theme park. The purpose of this guide is to provide *real* advice covering the many attractions, restaurants, and experiences from Universal Studios Hollywood and beyond.

Who are we? Well, we're theme park enthusiasts who spend a lot of time gathering first-hand knowledge and tips from all around the world. We've written guidebooks for Disneyland, Walt Disney World, Universal Orlando, and now we're tackling the fun of Universal Studios Hollywood! Advice from this guide is crafted from our trial and error—and now we're passing the fruit of our hard work on to you!

Keep in mind that this guide is an "unofficial edition," meaning it's not endorsed by with Universal Studios or its parent company. We are simply theme park goers who are giving an honest opinion on what the park has to offer. Though we call ourselves "fans" and do our best to keep a fun feel, we're also critical when necessary. Overall, we want this guide to be fun, fast, and informative!

FOR UNIVERSAL NEWBIES

If you've never been to Universal Studios Hollywood before, this book is perfect for you! We've crammed our guide with tidbits about the best food, attraction recommendations, secrets, family travel tips, and so much more. We'll fill you in on the theme park's lingo, history, and even its future. In the end, you'll have the knowledge of a pro!

FOR RETURN VISITORS

Universal Studios Hollywood is a constantly changing place. From exciting themed dining to upcoming thrilling attractions, *anything* could happen next!

If you haven't been to Universal Studios in ten years, this guide is a great fit. However, if you visit every month, you probably won't learn much. That, of course, doesn't mean that you won't learn *anything*, but you're likely already a pro and a guide to a park that's essentially your second home won't be much use. Still, if you're curious, we welcome you along for the ride! Even as often as we go, we still learned *a lot* from our research for this book.

Furthermore, if you've read our Disneyland Resort guide, this book may sound a bit repetitive. A lot of information in this guide is available (almost word-for-word) in our Disneyland book. However, this guide goes into much more detail!

A WORD FOR ALL

Since Universal Studios Hollywood updates so frequently, some of the items in this guide will change even weeks after its publication. Restaurants in CityWalk might close, attractions may be re-themed, popular food items could become discontinued... While most of this content should remain applicable to your trip, we just like to give you a heads up in case you notice a menu item change or an attraction closed for refurbishment.

A BRIEF HISTORY

Universal Studios Hollywood is much more than a theme park. In fact, it's still a very popular, fully working film and television production studio. For over 100 years, Universal Studios has produced famous films like Alfred Hitchcock's *The Birds* (1963), *Back to the Future* (1985), *Cast Away* (2000), and *Transformers* (2007). Famous actors, directors, and producers launched their careers here, so the production studios hold an incredible amount of fond memories.

Beginning in 1915, Universal Studios Hollywood hosted tours in the backlot for eager Hollywood hopefuls and curious tourists. At the time, guests could applaud for their favorite movie actors as filming took place and even boo at the villains as they walked on set. Since early filming took place during the silent era, the sound wasn't captured. However, once audio became prevalent in films, quiet sets began, and the tours eventually stopped.

It wasn't until 1964 that the studio would transform into a theme park. Guests eventually hopped aboard guided trams that detailed set locations and more. To lure visitors, elements were added around the tram like a petting zoo, stage shows, and new scenes with special effects.

Eventually, Universal's revamped theme park brought guests into the treacherous waters of the movie *Jaws*, the past with *Back to the Future*: The Ride, and even face-to-face with King Kong. After the opening of Universal Studios Florida in the 1990s, even more rides debuted at Universal Studios Hollywood. Many of these attractions used 3-D motion simulators and live entertainment shows based on popular films. Currently, Transformers: The Ride, Despicable Me: Minion Mayhem, and The Simpsons: The Ride, all use motion simulation with enormous screens and automated moving seats to propel guests into storylines.

With over 9 million visitors in recent years, Universal Studios Hollywood is one of the most visited theme parks in the world. With an iconic history, groundbreaking attractions, and an ideal Los Angeles location, Universal Studios Hollywood is an unforgettable time for movie and theme park fans.

PHRASES AROUND UNIVERSAL

General Admission – A one-day ticket to Universal Studios Hollywood. Experience all of the rides and shows within the theme park at no additional cost. The Studio Tour tram is included with this ticket. However, parking is at an extra cost per vehicle.

Universal Express Pass – For an additional cost, guests can buy their way to the front of the lines. Express Pass allows guests to skip the lines for each ride and show—once per ride, per day.

Single Rider Line – A fast way to get on the rides as long as you don't mind going without your party. Not every ride has this feature, but the popular ones often do.

Universal Studios Hollywood App – An Apple and Android application that allows you to check ride wait times, dining options, and show times.

CityWalk – A shopping and dining area located outside of the theme park.

Universal Team Member – An employee working at Universal Studios Hollywood.

Dark Ride – An indoor ride set in a dark building.

3D – The use of 3D glasses during the ride or attraction.

4D – The use of 3D glasses with added effects like splashing water and rumbling seats.

Animatronic – Robotic characters typically used in stage shows and rides.

Halloween Horror Nights (HHN) – A scary, horror-filled takeover of Universal Studios. Walk through mazes filled with actors playing murderers and monsters. This popular event is a secondary ticket price and shows from mid-September to early November.

⋆ **Magic Tips** ⋆

Throughout this book, we feature special insider tricks and secrets for planning your vacation. We call these "Magic Tips" and they are presented in boxes like this. Magic Tips are designed to:

- Save time waiting in lines
- Help you get the best show viewing
- Save money when booking

...and many other useful hacks!

RIDE LEVELS

Everyone – Perfect for all ages
Family – Suited for families with kids
Young Kids – Children ages 2-5
Kids – Children ages 6-9
Tweens – Children ages 10-12
Teens – Young people ages 13-17
Adults – People ages 18+
Thrill Riders – Those looking for the maximum thrill with attractions like roller coasters

RESOURCES

General – For booking and reservations:
www.UniversalStudiosHollywood.com

Customer Service – Booking and general questions:
1 (866) 258-6546

Our Website – For updates future updates to our Universal Studios Hollywood guide: **www.magicguidebooks.com**

CHAPTER ONE

PLANNING YOUR VACATION

PLANNING WHEN TO VISIT

Theme parks are incredibly popular in Southern California. From Disneyland to Universal Studios to Six Flags Magic Mountain, millions of locals visit these destinations each year.

As you may expect, weekends, holidays, and summers remain the busiest times to visit Universal. During these times, waits for rides are longer and walkways become packed. Dining spots in CityWalk may have lines out the door and parking garages quickly fill.

Furthermore, the addition of the Wizarding World of Harry Potter has increased Universal Studios Hollywood's popularity. After opening in 2016, record-breaking crowds have poured into the park to take part in the magic and experience the thrilling rides.

If a crowded theme park sounds like a nightmare to you, don't worry. Many of our readers only visit during these "peak" dates when schools are out of session and the weather is warmer. To combat the crowds, we offer crowd-beating tips and tricks we use ourselves.

MOST RECOMMENDED MONTHS

1. **September**
   Summer weather continues throughout September in Southern California. Expect far fewer crowds than in June, July, and August. Halloween decorations cover Universal Studios Hollywood for most of the month. The popular Halloween Horror Nights also begins in the middle of September. While the weekends for this event will be packed, the weekdays have the thinnest crowds.

2. **February**
   Universal typically has the fewest crowds at this time, even on the weekends. February also has cooler weather, and less expensive hotel rates. However, popular rides may go under refurbishment during this month.

3. **November**
   Like February, November is one of the least crowded months to visit Universal Studios Hollywood. Though theme park hours are limited, the crowds are so thin that even the most popular rides won't have wait times. However, Thanksgiving week is usually very, very busy.

LEAST-RECOMMENDED MONTHS

1. **July**
   Massive crowds from all over the world flood Los Angeles during July. Expect long lines and the hottest weather of the year.

2. **December**
   While park guests are treated to holiday decor and special attractions, the crowds are some of the most massive. If you must go in December, we recommend the first week.

3. **August**
   Like July, August is packed with tourists visiting during

their summer break. Expect crowds, hot days, and longer wait times for nearly every ride.

Note: If you're planning a visit during a crowded time of year, be sure to follow one of our pre-planned attraction lists. We use these lists ourselves and they can save you hours of time waiting in lines—or help you avoid them altogether.

DAY BREAKDOWN

Sunday
Weekend crowds, but far less than Saturday.

Monday
Often Mondays can be just as crowded as Sundays because guests take off extra days to avoid weekend traffic. Mondays directly after a holiday can also be very packed.

Tuesday
Our most recommended day for fewest crowds and the shortest lines.

Wednesday
Our second most recommended day for fewest crowds and the shortest lines.

Thursday
Third most recommended day for fewest crowds, but still busier than most Tuesdays and Wednesdays.

Friday
Less busy in the morning, but busiest in the evening after school when the locals tend to visit. CityWalk can be open later but gets swamped with locals experiencing the nightlife.

Saturday
By far, the busiest day at the theme park.

BEST DAYS TO VISIT

These days always depend on the month, but this is a general idea of how to avoid the largest crowds.

1. The 1st or 2nd weeks in February (especially Tuesdays and Wednesdays)
2. The last week in January (unless it's near the Martin Luther King Jr. Day holiday on the 3rd Monday of January)
3. Second week of September (but not around Labor Day)

MORE DATES TO CONSIDER

Weekdays – Like we said before, weekdays are the best times to plan your trip!

Holidays – These are the busiest times to visit because everyone has them off. Here is the list of holidays:

- Christmas (all week)
- New Year's (all week)
- Thanksgiving (all week)
- Easter (all week)
- The 4th of July (all week)
- Memorial Day weekend
- Labor Day weekend

- Martin Luther King Jr. weekend
- Presidents' Day weekend
- Columbus Day
- Veteran's Day weekend
- Mother's Day
- Father's Day (even more crowed than Mother's Day)

MONTH BREAKDOWN

JANUARY

Overview: January's crowd levels are split in two. The first half of the month is generally very crowded due to holiday crowds that carry over after Christmas. However, once schools are back in session, crowds don't resume until Martin Luther King, Jr. Day weekend.
Weather: Mid-60˚F (15˚C) during the day and chilly at night.
Least Crowded Days: The last week in January.
Most Crowded Days: The first two weeks (especially around New Year's) and Martin Luther King Jr. Weekend (Friday through Monday).

SPECIAL EVENT: EVE (NEW YEAR'S)
December 31, 2024 - January 1, 2025
Universal Studios Hollywood throws an annual New Year's celebration called EVE. The event typically takes place from 9PM - 2AM and hosts live DJs, photo ops, and fireworks! Limited tickets are available for EVE, so ride and show wait times are generally short. Tickets are usually around $130; food, champaign, cocktails, and beer are available for an additional cost. Tickets: UniversalStudiosHollywood.com

· Magic Tips ·
Special VIP passes for EVE are usually available for about $379. These passes include access to a VIP lounge, reserved viewing of the fireworks, and a buffet. Drinks with alcohol come at an additional cost. The VIP area also comes with front-of-the-line access (Express Pass), so if you want to completely skip the lines, this option could be for you. Just book early to avoid missing out as VIP tickets are limited.

SPECIAL EVENT: LUNAR NEW YEAR
Early 2024
Celebrate Lunar New Year at Universal Studios Hollywood with special food, decor, and entertainment. Characters from Kung Fu Panda and even a Mandarin-speaking Megaton from *Transformers* greet park guests. Most of the events take place in the Upper Lot where cherry blossom trees, lanterns, and photo ops decorate the plaza. We highly recommend checking out the snack booths for Lunar New Year as the Asian-inspired bites are usually very tasty. The entertainment is included with general admission, but the specialty food is a separate cost.

FEBRUARY

Overview: Possibly the least crowded month to visit Universal Studios Hollywood. Like January, the weather is cooler, but February is subject to attraction closures for refurbishment.
Weather: Low-70°F (21°C) during the day and chilly at night. February has been known to have sudden heatwaves, bringing the weather above 85°F (29°C).
Least Crowded Days: Any week except near Presidents' Day week.
Most Crowded Days: President's Day week

MARCH

Overview: March's popularity has increased recently as spring breaks spread throughout the month. Southern Californians generally don't like cold weather (which, to them, is anything below 65 degrees), so March is busier on warmer days. Expect weekends to have much larger crowds than weekdays.
Weather: mid-70°F (21°C) during the day and chilly at night, but March has been known to have occasional heatwaves, bringing the weather above 90°F (32°C).
Least Crowded Days: the first Tuesday, Wednesday, and Thursday of March.
Most Crowded: Last two weeks of the month for Spring Break.

APRIL

Overview: During April, spring breaks continue to pump crowds into Universal Studios Hollywood. Expect lighter crowds at the end of the month.
Weather: Mid-70°F (21°C) during the day and chilly at night.
Least Crowded Days: The last two weeks of the month.
Most Crowded Days: The weeks before and after Easter.

MAY

Overview: As Los Angeles warms in May and rainstorms become less frequent, Universal Studios starts to experience summer crowds. Furthermore, as college graduations take place, visiting families often pack the park on the weekends.

Weather: Mid-70°F (21°C) during the day and sometimes chilly after sunset.
Least Crowded Days: The first two weeks of the month.

Most Crowded Days: Memorial Day weekend (Friday through Tuesday).

GRAD BASH
Universal Studios Hollywood hosts special celebrations for graduating high school seniors in May and June. These events typically lead to larger crowds, especially in the evening. Most Grad Bash events run from 8PM - 12AM on select nights, including early park admission beginning at 5PM. Typically, these nights are weekdays.
For more information and date announcements, visit: https://www.universalyouthprograms.com/graduation/

JUNE

Overview: This month is known for "June Gloom" in Southern California. A thick, gray blanket of clouds will block out the sun until the afternoon on most days, though the temperature may be warm.
Weather: Mid-80°F (27°C) during the day. Typically cools at night.
Least Crowded Days: Tuesdays, Wednesdays, and Thursdays and the first week of the month.
Most Crowded Days: The last week of the month.

⋆ **Magic Tips** ⋆
Though Super Nintendo World will open earlier in the year, we expect it to be very popular during the summer. Expect larger-than-usual crowds throughout the season.

JULY

Overview: The weather heats up (sometimes unbearably so)

and crowds from all over the world visit Los Angeles. If you are planning to visit in July, we highly recommend our tips for beating the crowds at the end of this chapter.
Weather: High-80°F (27°C) during the day. Typically keeps warm at night.
Least Crowded Days: Tuesdays, Wednesdays, and Thursdays (unless one is July 4th)
Most Crowded Days: July 4th weekend

FOURTH OF JULY
See dazzling fireworks at several locations throughout the theme park and CityWalk around 9:30PM. Parking gets packed during this time, so get to the parks in the morning to secure a spot. Leaving may also be difficult, so you may want to hang out at CityWalk for an hour afterward to avoid the rush.

AUGUST

Overview: The weather continues to heat up even more in August as crowds continue through the middle of the month.
Weather: Mid-90°F (32°C) during the day. Typically keeps very warm at night.
Least Crowded Days: Tuesdays, Wednesdays, and Thursdays, and the last two weeks of the month.
Most Crowded Days: The first two weeks of the month.

SEPTEMBER

Overview: Hot summer weather continues through September as Halloween celebrations begin. Labor Day weekend (September 3-6) brings large crowds.
Weather: High-90°F (32°C) during the day. Typically keeps very warm at night.
Least Crowded Days: Tuesdays, Wednesdays, Thursdays, and Fridays.
Most Crowded Days: Labor Day weekend.

OCTOBER

Overview: Halloween fans will want to visit during this month! However, Universal's Halloween isn't for the squeamish. The popular Halloween Horror Nights is a separate ticketed nighttime event with terrifying mazes, plenty of gore, and horror franchises brought to life! We detail Halloween Horror Nights in a separate chapter later in this guide.

Weather: Low-80°F (27°C) during the day, cools at night.

Least Crowded Days: Tuesdays, Wednesdays, and Thursdays.

Most Crowded Days: Evenings when guests visit before Halloween Horror Nights.

> **· Magic Tips ·**
> Halloween Horror Nights occurs on select dates throughout September and October. Due to this, normal park hours usually conclude by 6PM each day. If you're planning a visit in October, be sure to make note of this as it could affect your day planning.

NOVEMBER

Overview: The holidays don't begin until after Thanksgiving at Universal Studios Hollywood. However, crowds pack the park around Veterans Day (November 11) and the entire week of Thanksgiving.

Weather: Mid-70°F (21°C) during the day, cools at night to 50°F (10°C).

Least Crowded Days: The first week of the month.

Most Crowded: Veteran's Day weekend and Thanksgiving week.

DECEMBER

Overview: The holidays are in full gear at Universal Studios Hollywood. See decorations, purchase special treats, and meet holiday characters like the Grinch!
Weather: Low-60°F (15°C) during the day, can cool at night to mid-40°F (5°C).
Least Crowded Days: The first week of the month.
Most Crowded: The last two weeks, especially Christmas Day and New Year's Eve.

SPECIAL EVENT: CHRISTMAS
Mid-November – Early January
See the glimmering Christmas lights that dazzle around Universal Studios Hollywood! Christmas trees, ornaments, and garland make this a season to remember. Just be sure to stick around after dark to see the lights!

⋆ Magic Tips ⋆
Southern California theme parks become incredibly busy during the holiday season. Even after Christmas concludes, expect record crowds from December 26-31. If you're visiting during this time, we highly recommend writing down your day plan and backup options in case restaurants and experiences become too crowded.

HOLIDAY ATTRACTIONS

- **Hogsmeade Village** – The Wizarding World of Harry Potter transforms with special decorations and the stunning nighttime light show, The Magic of Christmas at Hogwarts Castle.
- **Holiday Food** – Many restaurants and snack locations serve special holiday food during this time.

- **Grinchmas** – The Grinch, his dog, Max, and characters from Who-ville arrive for Grinchmas. This annual event has music and photo ops to celebrate the holidays. There's also a stage show in front of a 65-foot, Dr. Seuss-style tree that magically lights each night! Kids especially love this lively event!
- **CityWalk** – Shop for presents and try seasonal dishes at many of the spots around CityWalk.

· Magic Tips ·
We're a little vague on details here because Universal Studios' holiday lineup changes from year to year. However, most of the experiences should stay relatively the same.

BEAT THE CROWDS

1. **Get There Early** – We can't stress this tip enough. Most of the locals stroll in an hour or two after the park opens, so getting there early gives you access to the rides without the waits.

2. **Make a Plan** – Avoid the lines by following one of our pre-planned attraction lists found at the end of this guide. Each plan is based on interest and/or age group to maximize your time at the park.

3. **Avoid Busy Lunch and Dinner** – On busy days, eat lunch after 1:30pm and dinner before 5:30pm or after 7:30pm. You can also reserve a table at select restaurants in CityWalk. We list those in the dining section of this guide.

4. **Splash Early** – Universal Studios Hollywood's only water ride, Jurassic World—The Ride, becomes especially busy on hot days. To avoid the long lines, experience it before 11AM. Afterward, you can dry off in the hot afternoon sun as you walk around the park!

5. **Use Early Park Admission (if available)** – Since Universal Studios Hollywood doesn't have its own resort hotels like Disneyland, the theme park sometimes partners with nearby hotels for promotions. During select times, guests staying at these hotels may have early entry into parts of the park, including The Wizarding World of Harry Potter. If you have Early Park Admission, be sure to take advantage and beat the daytime crowds.

6. **Accept the Wait** – Waiting in line isn't the end of the world. Sometimes we all have to do it for the best attractions. The trick is to wait the *shortest* amount of time for the *fewest* rides possible. You can avoid the longest lines by following our planned-out ride lists.

7. **Take a Break** – The worst thing you can do on your vacation is exhaust yourself. If you are feeling worn out, take a break by watching a show or visiting Universal CityWalk. After you've recharged, head back into the park to complete your ride list.

· Magic Tips ·

If you can't get to the theme parks early, plan to stay late! Just like the morning hours, late nights often have shorter wait times. However, this only works when the park is open late during peak seasons such as summer and holidays.

MORE PLANNING TIPS

Packing the right things for your day at a theme park is essential. Otherwise, you may end up sunburnt and spending a small fortune on bottles of water. However, you also don't want to overpack, so we've created this list to help you prepare.

WHAT TO BRING

1. **What to Wear** – Shorts, t-shirts, sneakers (trainers), and tank tops are seen all around the resort for a good reason: they are comfortable. You'll spend a lot of time outdoors, walking around the theme park, so we recommend that you dress comfortably. Even on a hot day, Los Angeles can get chilly at night. We also recommend taking a jacket or sweater to keep you warm during the winter.

2. **Hats and Sunglasses** – It's sunny Southern California, so protecting our face is necessary. However, you should be careful of hats and sunglasses on rides so as not to lose them. Luckily, many thrill rides have places to store your belongings.

3. **Sunscreen** – Even on a cloudy day, the ultraviolet rays from the sun can give you an uncomfortable burn. Be careful and stay protected—you don't want to ruin your vacation with a terrible sunburn.

4. **Small Bag** – If you have several items to carry or plan to buy souvenirs, we recommend carrying a small bag with you. Drawstring backpacks work the best as they can fit into most of the free lockers. Also, keep in mind that your bag will be checked by security before entering the park area.

5. **Stroller** – You can bring your own or rent one at one of the parks. If you're even a little worried that your child may be too tired to walk around all day, it's best to use caution and set aside extra cash for a stroller rental. Single strollers are $15 a day and doubles are $25.

6. **Water Bottles and Snacks** – You can save money (or help any picky eaters in your party) by bringing your own snacks. Thankfully, Universal Studios allows you to bring sealed bottles of water into the parks. However, if you don't mind fountain water, you can refill your bottle at water fountains near any restroom for free.

7. **Money** – Universal Studios Hollywood accepts all major credit cards and cash.

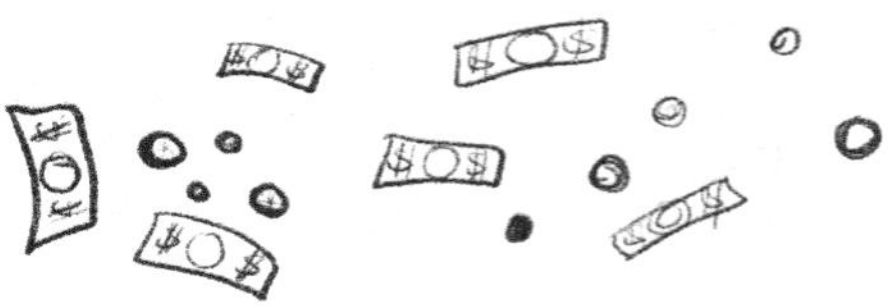

8. **Identification** – For adults, make sure you plan on bringing your government-issued ID if you plan to drink alcoholic beverages. You may be asked to present ID when purchasing at shops in CityWalk as well.

9. **Hand Sanitizer** – After the outbreak of COVID-19, washing your hands is critical to maintaining health. You'll likely touch handrails, seat cushions, and many other things that will require you to disinfect before touching food. However, hand sanitizer should only be used if warm water and soap aren't easily available.

10. **Extra Phone Charger** – If you have a smartphone, we highly recommend an extra portable charger. We also recommend becoming familiar enough with your smartphone so that you can turn on the battery-saver

mode in the settings. This will prevent you from running out of juice too early while you take pictures and use the Universal Studios app.

11. **Waterproof Bag** – If you plan on riding the water attractions—like Jurassic World—you're likely to get wet. The last thing you want is to accidentally drench your cellphone! If your device isn't water resistant, bring a plastic sandwich bag for each phone to keep them dry (this also works great for wallets).

12. **Simple Rain Gear** – It doesn't rain much in Los Angeles (only around 15 inches of rainfall per year), but just in case it does, compact umbrellas and ponchos are great ways to stay dry.

BACKUP PLANS

RENT A LOCKER

If you don't feel like lugging around a backpack all day, rent a locker just outside of the park gates near the restrooms. Lockers are also available near Harry Potter & the Forbidden Journey, The Mummy, and Jurassic World. There's also a locker room located in CityWalk near Hot Topic. Day rental prices range from $8-$15 per locker.

REPLACEMENT ITEMS

If you forget any items, Universal Studios Hollywood likely sells them. Check the gift shops after the theme park entrance or the Universal Store in CityWalk.

UNIVERSAL HOLLYWOOD APP

Universal Studios developed a free mobile application for accessing important information around the parks. See wait times for popular attractions, a map of the theme parks, park hours, and even access a "virtual line" for certain rides like Secret Life of Pets: Off the Leash.

Universal offers free in-park Wi-Fi for its guests using the app. To access this, connect to "UNIVERSAL" on the list of available networks in your Wi-Fi settings. Once connected, open your internet browser and follow the instructions to gain approval.

In the app, you can also create your own itinerary and check items off as you go. While this feature is a little clunky, it does help with organizing on the go.

⋆ **Magic Tips** ⋆
We highly recommend downloading the app before you visit the park to familiarize yourself with its functions. That way, if it's a busy day, you're not dealing with crowds and trying to figure out the app.

PANDEMIC CHANGES

In the spring of 2021, Universal Studios Hollywood reopened after over a year of closures. When the park reopened, guests ages 2 and older were required to wear a mask while visiting. Masks needed to be properly fitting, not contain holes, and be made of breathable material. However, most health and safety measures were eventually relaxed or stopped altogether within the next year.

In the event that local, state, or federal guidelines change for public events, we may see mandatory masks return for all theme park guests. We also may see physical distancing be enforced around Universal Studios Hollywood and CityWalk. This could include separating parties with markers on the ground in the queues. Furthermore, indoor queuing, dining, and shopping may be limited. In fact, the total park capacity could be restricted. In this event, Universal Studios Hollywood would likely use a reservation system for guests with tickets.

Finally, some experiences could be modified or not open to guests. This could include rides, dining, and other attractions. Whatever the case, we also expect Universal Studios to increase cleaning around the park and encourage guests to regularly wash their hands.

Of course, we're only giving you this information as a planning precaution. All safety measures will be posted on UniversalStudiosHollywood.com.

CHAPTER TWO

BOOKING YOUR TRIP

TIPS BEFORE YOU BOOK

Universal Studios Hollywood is home to many attractions, but most trips can be fully covered in a day. Some choose to extend to two days, but we don't recommend more than that. There simply aren't enough experiences to warrant a longer trip. For those staying longer, we cover other experiences in Southern California later in this guide.

PRE-BOOK YOUR HOTEL

Unlike Disneyland or Universal Studios Orlando, Hollywood doesn't have a set of dedicated hotels. The only official hotel is run by Sheraton and it's just outside of the theme park. Wherever you choose to stay, we recommend pre-booking at least 3 months in advance to get the best deals.

PLANNING TRAVEL

You can drive, fly, and shuttle to Universal Studios Hollywood. Since it's smack-dab in the middle of Los Angeles, there are plenty of transportation options to explore. In the next chapter, review the best ways to travel to the theme park.

PURCHASING TICKETS

BUNDLE FOR BIGGER SAVINGS

Sometimes purchasing a flight/hotel/car package from a third-party travel site can save you money. However, bundling theme park tickets with travel typically isn't much of a discount.

KNOW THE TICKET PRICE STRUCTURE

Universal Studios uses a date-based ticket pricing structure. Similar to airlines and hotels, prices are higher or lower depending on your visiting date. In this case, weekends, summer, Christmas, and other holidays tend to have the most expensive pricing. Conversely, weekdays and off-peak months like February have the lowest prices.

⋆ **Magic Tips** ⋆

We highly recommend purchasing tickets before your visit. Not only will you save a little versus the front gate pricing, but you'll also avoid long lines to purchase tickets.

OTHER TICKETS

Universal also offers special tickets with enhanced experiences. The Universal Express pass allows guests to cut the line, once per attraction, throughout the day. The VIP Experience is an exclusive tour throughout the studios where you can stage photo ops and cut the line to most attractions. VIP also comes with snacks and drinks during your visit. Keep in mind that both of these options cost a lot of money—as much as 3-4 times the normal day ticket.

TICKET PRICING

TICKET TYPE	ADULT (10+)	CHILD (3-9)
1-Day General Admission	$109 - $149	$103 - $143
2-Day General Admission	$149 - $189	$143 - $183
Universal Express Pass (add-on)	$199 - $309	$199 - $309
VIP Experience	$369 and up	$369 and up

Children 2 and under receive free entry to all experiences with a paying adult. However, children must be 5 years or older for the VIP Experience. Teens must be at least 17 years old for the tour without an adult.

⋆ Magic Tips ⋆
California Residents can sometimes save on admission and Universal Express Pass when purchasing in advance. It's usually around 10% off of standard prices.

EXPRESS PASS TIPS

For many new visitors, the thought of waiting in line at a theme park feels exhausting. So it's only natural to consider splurging on an Express Pass for the day. However, a family of four could spend over $1,000 on these add-on tickets alone. Before forking over the dough, you may want to review a few things:

TIPS BEFORE BUYING EXPRESS PASS

1. **Consider the Crowds** – If you're visiting on a weekday in September, you likely won't need Express Pass. By this

time, most family vacations have ended and so the crowds are much thinner. Even if you visit on a weekend in May, wait times may not warrant the money.

⋆ **Magic Tips** ⋆
Our Month Breakdown in the previous chapter reviews crowd levels and date recommendations. Additionally, Universal's ticket prices will be higher for busier days and lower for ones with fewer crowds.

2. **Buy Ahead** – Express Passes are usually cheaper when booked ahead on UniversalStudiosHollywood.com.

3. **Limited Experiences** – To keep the Express Pass lines short, Universal Studios only distributes a limited number of passes per day. It's hard to know when the theme park might run out of passes, but busier days tend to sell out sometimes weeks in advance.

4. **You Can Still Buy There** – If you arrive and the lines for rides are too long, you may still be able to buy Express Pass. Visit one of the many store locations around Universal for this add-on offer—if passes haven't sold out!

VIP EXPERIENCE REVIEW

The VIP Experience at Universal Studios Hollywood is designed for those wanting a closer, exclusive look at the studio backlot. While VIP also offers cut-the-line privileges, the experience is mostly designed around the studio portion.

With that said, if you're interested in up-close looks at real Hollywood sets, this tour is fantastic. Throughout the day, you'll learn fascinating history from Universal tour guides about iconic films and television series shot at Universal. Even better, the tour encourages you to snap photos on locations like the clock tower from *Back to the Future*!

The tour requires quite a bit of walking outdoors, but there are several portions that involve a small tram. Furthermore, this tram feels much more exclusive than the standard Hollywood Backlot tour. For many, the standard tram is a satisfying peek at the backlot, but it seats hundreds of guests at a time, so the experience isn't personalized. Conversely, VIP offers plenty of one-on-one time as you're rarely in a group larger than a couple dozen other guests. The standard tour also doesn't allow guests to leave the tram and wander the sets as VIP does.

The VIP Experience includes up-close parking, special VIP check-in, breakfast, bottled water, an exclusive tour of the backlot, Express Pass privileges, and lunch. The meals work like a catered buffet with several hot and cold options. Food here is great and you can certainly eat your fill if desired.

Universal does a fantastic job of making guests feel like a true Hollywood VIP for the day with this experience. We don't recommend waiting until the day of to purchase, as time slots could fill. Also keep in mind that Universal could change any of these experiences during your visit. For example, the website lists one meal and snacks with your visit. However, we've noticed that most VIP tours include much more than that.

Book your experience online or upgrade to the Private VIP Experience by calling (818) 622-8477. The private experience is designed for one group or family and prices vary per date.

TICKET DISCOUNTS

There are many ways to save when booking a visit to Universal Studios Hollywood. Generally, booking in advance is the easiest way to save. We've gathered some helpful places to score the best deals.

UNIVERSALSTUDIOSHOLLYWOOD.COM

The theme park's official website is the easiest way to get tickets. You can purchase general admission, Express Pass, VIP, and annual passes on the site. Online tickets are also about $10 cheaper than if you buy them at the gate. Purchasing ahead also allows you to skip the ticket lines and head straight to the theme park entrance.

MILITARY DISCOUNTS

Discounted tickets for members of the military (active, retired, or disabled) can save on tickets at Military Offices nationwide. If you don't pre-purchase a ticket, bring your military ID to the ticket booth and receive an additional $3 off each purchased ticket.

ANNUAL PASSES

Universal Studios Hollywood offers annual passes (APs) for those who frequent the theme park every year. Some passes have "blockout dates" during busy times, meaning that the pass will not be valid on those days.

Depending on the pass type, you may have special perks that come with your annual pass. For example, the Gold AP comes with complimentary parking, as does the Platinum AP. However, both of these passes are more expensive than the Silver AP that does not come with included parking. It's important to review these price differences before purchasing as well as the blockout dates. With parking at Universal Studios costing $30 per vehicle, it may make sense to purchase the Gold pass over the Silver one, as it could save you money in the long run.

· Magic Tips ·
Universal Studios Hollywood annual passes grant admission to the park during regular theme park hours. Most do not give access for special events like Halloween Horror Nights (Platinum Annual Passes get a free ticket to Horror Nights). However, you may receive a discount for attending one or more of these events.

PROS OF UNIVERSAL ANNUAL PASSES

1. Visit Multiple Times – APs allow guests to return on several dates throughout the year!

2. Discounts – Some passes have discounts on dining, select snacks, merchandise, and special events. Furthermore, these discounts can be used on alcohol, at CityWalk, and in most retail locations, depending on availability.

3. Payment Plan – Universal offers interest-free monthly payments after an initial down payment.

4. Advanced Event Purchase – AP members get first dibs on select event tickets before they go on sale to the public.

5. Exclusives – Discounted or complimentary items such as snacks and merchandise are available seasonally for annual passholders. Universal communicates these deals via their email newsletter.

6. Free Parking – Gold and Platinum Annual Passes come with included parking during your visit.

· Magic Tips ·

Universal offers a wide variety of annual passes, depending on the location of purchase. For example, Costco members may purchase a Silver Annual Pass with different blockout dates than those who purchase on UniversalStudiosHollywood.com. So, even though two passes are both the "Silver" level, they could have slightly different benefits.

CONS OF UNIVERSAL ANNUAL PASSES

1. Blockout Dates – The less expensive annual passes have the most blockout dates. So if you want to visit during the summer, many weekends, or holidays, you'll need to pay more money.
2. Parking Cost – If your pass doesn't include parking, you'll have to pay for each visit. Depending on how many trips you make, this can really add up!

PASS TYPES

SILVER ANNUAL PASS

$239

With less blockout dates than a Neighbor Pass, the Silver works for those needing more weekend availability for their visit. Perks include over 60 weekend days, small discounts for friends/family, Halloween Horror Nights discounted tickets, and special events access. Guests can also use the Silver Pass on any first date, even if the pass is blocked.

GOLD ANNUAL PASS

$319

Get the benefits of a Silver Pass, but with fewer blockout dates! Gold pass members also receive complimentary general parking before 6pm, and 15% off food, beverages, and merchandise.

PLATINUM ANNUAL PASS

$629

Get full access to the park with no blockout dates, free general parking before 6pm, and Express Pass after 3pm, and a free Halloween Horror Nights ticket, 15% off food, beverages, merchandise—and more!

· **Magic Tips** ·

General admission tickets can often be upgraded to Annual Passes by visiting the box office before leaving. However, you can save even more money when purchasing beforehand on Universal's website. Early purchase discounts range from $15-$60, depending on the pass.

CALIFORNIA NEIGHBOR PASS

$189

At times, Universal Studios Hollywood may offer special passes for just residents of California. These are discounted

APs with several blockout dates. Some of these passes may only work seasonally, offering visits for part of the year.

For more AP information, details, and purchasing, visit: https://store.universalstudioshollywood.com/PurchaseTickets.aspx

CHAPTER THREE

TRAVELING TO UNIVERSAL STUDIOS

INTRODUCTION

Now that we've covered booking your visit, it's time to begin your vacation to Universal Studios Hollywood. Getting there doesn't have to be tricky, but if you don't plan correctly, it could feel very stressful.

The theme park is located in Universal City, just outside of Hollywood. Whether you're flying, driving, or taking another form of transport, we have tips for your arrival. In this chapter, we review the several different methods of getting to the resort. How you get there is entirely up to you, but if you're feeling indecisive (or just need more information in order to choose), read thoroughly to review the best choices.

BY AIRLINE

If you aren't planning a road trip and live far away from Los Angeles, flying will likely be your quickest method. While airlines can be expensive at times, there are several ways to save money:

1. Compare airlines to see the best pricing.
2. Check baggage fees and allowed carry-on items. If you live on the East Coast, Spirit Airlines is an *à la carte* option

that can save you hundreds of dollars, especially on last-minute flights.

3. Book early, if you can, to get the best discounts.

NEARBY AIRPORTS

If you are planning to fly to Los Angeles, we recommend LAX (Los Angeles International airport) or Burbank. LAX is a major airport located right next to highways that will take you directly to Hollywood. Burbank Airport is much smaller and within a 20-minute drive to Universal Studios. However, you may find different airfare depending on the airport. If you're planning on renting a car, the airports also have several choices for car companies. We discuss transportation in the next chapter.

FLIGHTS WITHIN THE U.S.A.

SOUTHWEST

We recommend Southwest because the staff is friendly, the seats are comfortable, and flights include complimentary snacks, soft drinks, and two free checked luggage bags per person. Free bags are very hard to find these days in the United States, so this is a great deal!

If you book during Southwest's "Wanna Get Away" deals, you can score some great rates. Southwest works perfectly if you book ahead when these deals are available. However, if you are late to the game, tickets can get pretty pricey.

> **⋆ Magic Tips ⋆**
> Southwest typically "drops" its best deals on Tuesdays and they sometimes expire by Thursday of the same week. If possible, avoid booking on weekends so you don't miss these deals.

Southwest offers first-come-first-served seating, which has its pros and cons. We highly recommend paying the extra money to get the "Early Bird" option. This will allow everyone in your party to pick seats together for your flight. Before boarding, you can ask their helpful staff members to assist with seating your family together, though it can't be guaranteed.

Southwest also doesn't charge for change fees. So, if you have to switch or cancel your flight for whatever reason, you can do so without extra charge. There are limitations to these changes and funds are returned to you as travel credits.

ALASKA

We recommend Alaska Airlines for its updated aircrafts and well-rounded service. Book early enough and their rates are very affordable. Alaska gives you the free option to select your seat, but checked bags are often at a moderately priced additional charge. Alaska also offers free soft drinks and snacks for their flights. From the West Coast, Alaska is usually one of the few airlines that offers nonstop flights. If you've never flown Alaska, we invite you to give them a try!

DELTA

Delta is a premium airline that excels in what it does. The service, aircrafts, and professionalism with this airline are consistent and top-notch. While Delta isn't as innovative with its deals as Southwest, it does deliver plenty of flight options.

However, those traveling from the West Coast may be able to find fantastic deals when flying Delta to Los Angeles. Conversely, longer flights cost a pretty penny. If you're able to find an affordable deal with Delta, we'd recommend booking with them.

· Magic Tips ·

Airlines like Alaska and Delta offer discounted "economy" fares for many of their flights. These prices are low—and very tempting. We typically book economy for last-minute flights. However, economy fares come with several restrictions. You may not have a seat selection choice or a guarantee that you'll sit with your party. However, Alaska usually allows economy guests to choose their seats. Others may charge an additional fee which ends up making the economy pricing a wash.

SPIRIT

This airline is an *à la carte* airline, so the first price you see is just for a seat on the plane—everything else is an extra fee. These fees include: picking your own seat, checking a bag or putting a bag in the overhead compartment, drinks, and snacks.

If you don't mind where you sit and only need to bring a personal item, Spirit can save you some big bucks. However, once you pick a seat and opt to bring another bag (even carry-on bags are extra), the prices begin to stack. Also, Spirit Airlines doesn't have much of a customer service department in our opinion.

We've had both smooth and rocky experiences with Spirit Airlines. Their flights can change gates seemingly without warning and the airline might take awhile to update their passengers. Just understand that you usually get what you pay for and Spirit is no exception to that rule.

FRONTIER

Works similarly to Spirit and can get to be very pricey. We find that Spirit tends to have more comfortable seats than Frontier. If you're only on a two-hour flight or less, you may not mind. Frontier is fine for last-minute flights if you're looking to save and don't need any extra pizazz. Just remember the checked bags are additional.

BY CAR

Unlike New York City, where public transportation methods are everywhere, Los Angeles pretty much depends on cars to get around. Furthermore, LA traffic is a notorious nightmare. We often joke that driving in LA takes no less than 30 minutes, even if you're traveling just 5 miles.

With that said, we recommend traveling by car in the city. Whether you rent a vehicle or use ridesharing, there's really no better option for getting around Los Angeles.

CAR RENTAL

We recommend Enterprise.com or Dollar.com for car rentals as they typically have a great selection and the best pricing. Pre-booking before you arrive at the airport is advised. Here are some popular car rental companies near LAX and Universal Studios:

- www.enterprise.com – You can visit the company's website or see typically better deals on Priceline.com (or bundle with your airfare and hotel booking).
- www.dollar.com – Click the "specials" tab for deals.
- www.budget.com – Click the "deals" tab for offers.

DRIVING TO UNIVERSAL STUDIOS

Universal Studios Hollywood is directly off the 101 Hollywood Freeway in Los Angeles. We highly recommend using a GPS app for the fastest route. Additionally, LA construction may reroute certain areas, so always look for detour signs when present.

However, GPS sometimes tells drivers to get off the road a little too early. Once you arrive to Universal Studios Blvd, follow the signs to the parking structures.

Driving from LAX to Universal takes anywhere from 30 to 60 minutes, depending on the time of day. If you want to avoid heavy traffic on the freeways, drive after 7PM during the week.

PARKING AT UNIVERSAL

Universal Studios Hollywood has several main parking structures for visiting guests. You won't be able to choose your structure, as guests are rerouted depending on availability. Once you've parked, walkways lead into the CityWalk shopping area. You must walk through CityWalk in order to get to the theme park gates.

· Magic Tips ·
Universal Studios Hollywood parking garages include Frankenstein, Jurassic Parking, ET Garage, Woody Woodpecker, and Curious George. The Curious George and ET parking structures are the furthest from the theme park and house most of the general parking. The Jurassic and Woody garages are dedicated to preferred parking and Frankenstein is for those paying to get Front Gate spots.

PARKING FEES

General Parking
$30 before 5PM ($10 after 5PM, excluding Halloween Horror Nights dates). General parking allows guests to park in most spots located around the parking structures at Universal Studios Hollywood. However, you will have to walk about 15-20 minutes before getting to the theme park.

Preferred Parking
$50 before 6PM ($20 after 5PM). Preferred parking saves a bit on walking and is great for busy days. However, we're not totally sold on preferred parking since it's a lot pricier than general parking and maybe cuts off 5 minutes of walking time. We'd recommend splurging on Front Gate parking if you want to be close.

Front Gate Parking
$60 to park all day near the gate. Park within a 5-minute walk to the theme park and have easy access to your vehicle throughout the day. If you're planning on packing your own

meals, this may be the way to go so that you don't lose too much time walking through CityWalk to your car.

Valet Parking
$25 for the first 2 hours, and $45 after. We don't see much use for Valet parking unless you have a vehicle that needs a special spot. It's not much more accessible than Preferred parking.

FREE SHUTTLE

Universal Studios offers a free shuttle for those arriving at the Metro station. A pedestrian bridge is located near these spots on the corner of Lankershim and Universal Hollywood Drive. One you've crossed the bridge, the shuttle takes guests to CityWalk. Even better, the theme park is just a 1-minute walk from the shuttle drop-off point.

BY METRO

The Metro B Line in Los Angeles stops at several favorite spots around the city. The LA Convention Center, Staples Center, Hollywood Walk of Fame, and Universal Studios are all included in this line.

If you're using the Metro Line, parking is just $3 per day at Universal Studios Hollywood. After that, use the free shuttle to arrive at the theme park.

Rates and passes are available at: https://www.metro.net/riding/guide/B-line.

⋆ **Magic Tips** ⋆
There are only about 500 parking spaces at the Metro Station near Universal Studios, so they fill up quickly. If you're planning on using one of these spots, arrive at least 45 minutes before park opening.

BY RIDESHARE OR TAXI

Ridesharing has quickly become one of the most popular forms of transportation around Los Angeles. Lyft and Uber are the most-used apps for this traveling method. If you're not familiar with these services, they are used to request a driver for transportation. However, these are everyday people rather than official taxis. You can also request larger and/or luxury vehicles for your travel, if needed. In the end, costs tend to lower and the experience is often friendlier than standard taxis.

To download one of these rideshare applications, open the App Store (Apple devices) or Play Store (Android devices) and search the application by its name. The time of day and traffic will influence the travel costs of rideshare apps.

If arriving by taxi, it's customary to tip your cab driver 15–20%. Of course, the tip amount always depends on your experience with the driver.

You won't have to pay for parking when using a rideshare service or taxi. The cars drop guests off at CityWalk and its about a 5-10 minute walk to the theme park from there.

⋆ **Magic Tips** ⋆

If you're dropping off passengers, look for the drop-off signs or ask a Team Member before parking. Most cars drop off in the same location on Level 1 of CityWalk. Cars have an easy way in and out of this drop-off zone without paying for parking.

CHAPTER FOUR

RIDES & ATTRACTIONS

INTRODUCTION

Universal Studios Hollywood is split into two levels: the Upper Lot and the Lower Lot. Most of the attractions are located in the Upper Lot and are split into "mini lands" based on several franchises. Harry Potter, The Simpsons, Despicable Me, and The Secret Life of Pets all have attractions based around these popular films and television series.

The Lower Lot is accessible via a set of escalators known as the Universal StarWay. It takes about 10 minutes to journey from the Upper Lot to the Lower Lot on the StarWay. The escalators have a shade covering and also bring guests back to the Upper Lot.

Popular rides are also located in the Lower Lot: a Jurassic World water ride, a 3D Transformers ride, and a Revenge of the Mummy indoor rollercoaster. Super Nintendo World expands the lower lot with interactive games, a colorful landscape, and the marquee Mario Kart: Bowser's Challenge.

Since Universal Studios Hollywood aims at bringing its guests into the movies, many of its attractions use motion simulation. This means the ride chair or vehicle moves along with a screen to simulate you driving, flying, crashing, and escaping action sequences.

In the past, the attractions at Universal mostly hit well with tweens to adults—especially those who love Harry Potter. Now, the theme park's experiences have been revved up to include attractions for small children. The Secret Life of Pets, Super Nintendo World, and a mini Despicable Me land all aim to entertain young ones.

⋆ **Magic Tips** ⋆
For many people, motion simulation makes them feel ill. If this includes you, we recommend spacing out these types of rides or skipping them altogether. As we describe the attractions throughout this chapter, we detail which use motion simulation as part of the experience.

UPPER LOT

WORLD-FAMOUS STUDIO TOUR

If there's one thing you do at Universal Studios, make sure it's the World-Famous Studio Tour. Hop aboard a large tram and visit actual Hollywood sets! The tram is guided by Jimmy Fallon on a screen and a live Universal Team Member. Starting in the Upper Lot, you'll drive through movie sets in the Wild West and New York. Some of the scenes recreate special effects used in film like flash floods, and there's even an appearance of the great white shark from *Jaws*!

Other exciting features of this hour-long tour include a trek into the jungle where King Kong lives and a high-speed chase in Fast & Furious: Supercharged. 3D glasses are encouraged for these sequences and add some extra thrill to the experience.

The Studio Tram is probably the best feature of Universal Studios Hollywood. The ability to visit real-life Hollywood sets is something the entire family will remember for years to come. Guests can also snap photos and take videos as they go. However, the tram may drive near a live set where guests are required to stay silent so as not to disrupt filming.

Ride Type: Tram tour with some 3D motion simulation elements. The tram doesn't go very fast, but some of the sequences simulate it doing so.

Level: Everyone, although kids under 8 may find some of the King Kong sequences frightening.

Height Restriction: None

Recommendation: An unforgettable 60-minute ride for anyone wishing to visit actual Hollywood film sets. Universal adds some thrills as part of this experiences as well as relays fun facts about Hollywood productions filmed there.

· Magic Tips ·

To better spot celebrities and live tapings, plan your tram tour on a weekday and in the late morning before lunchtime.

Keep in mind that live tapings may also shorten the experience. If a film set is being used, the tram stays clear of the area and the entire tour might be shortened due to this. If you want the entire tram tour experience, it's best to aim for visiting on the weekend.

The World-Famous Studio Tour also offers Spanish and Mandarin tours throughout the day.

THE SECRET LIFE OF PETS: OFF THE LEASH

Based on the popular animated film franchise, this dark ride takes guests through a hilarious and family-friendly journey. Max, Snowball, Gidget, and many other characters show up during the ride!

One of the few kid-friendly rides found in Universal, the attraction allows guests to feel like an adopted pet. As you navigate around the scenes, zany actions occur in this unique experience.

Ride Type: A slow-paced, family friendly dark ride

Level: Young Kids, Kids, Families

Height Restriction: 34" (87cm). Children must be at least 48" (122cm) to ride without an adult.

Virtual Line: This attraction sometimes uses a Virtual Line instead of a traditional queue. Guests may join the Virtual Line for free using the Universal Studios Hollywood app.

Recommendation: We recommend this ride for families with children 9 and under as the experience is tailored for them. However, all guests can enjoy this colorful and hilarious attraction.

⋆ **Magic Tips** ⋆

The Virtual Line sometimes does not appear on the app until an hour or so after the park opens. If you don't see the option, we recommend checking the app often. On slower days, the Virtual Line may not be needed. It's a little bit frustrating because you may not have a definite time when the Virtual Line will open. For this reason, we recommend heading to your first ride and continuously checking the app.

DREAMWORKS THEATRE FEATURING KUNG FU PANDA

Follow Po and his friends as they complete a fantastic quest using stunning visual effects. This theatre-in-the-round show has moving seats but is gentle enough for young kids to experience.

Ride Type: A movie theater show with moving seats, a wide projection screen, and special effects.

Level: Young Kids, Kids, Tweens

Height Restriction: None

Recommendation: This attraction has whimsical action, humor, and beautiful special effects. However, adults may not be as entertained. The storyline and effects are very cartoonish and aimed at children.

· **Magic Tips** ·
Children are not permitted to sit on the laps of adults in the moving seats. If you have a young child, ask a Universal Team Member to direct you to a stationary seat.

THE SIMPSONS RIDE

Description: The world's favorite cartoon family brings their crazy antics to this hilarious motion simulation ride. Although animation for The Simpsons Ride feels a bit dated, its still incredibly popular at the theme park. Several references from the show are found throughout the ride and the queue, however you don't need to be a Simpsons fan to enjoy this attraction.

Simpsons fans can also enjoy dining, shopping, and photo ops with characters outside of the ride. Visit Krusty Burger, the Kwik-E-Mart, and try a giant Lard Lad donut! We review the Simpsons-themed restaurants later in this guide.

Ride Type: Motion simulation with many ride vehicles sharing the same screen. Most of the attraction is computer animated.

Level: Tweens, Teens, Adults, Thrill Riders

Height Restriction: 40" (102cm). Children must be at least 48" (122cm) to ride without an adult.

Recommendation: The humor might be a little crude for young kids (or it may go over their heads entirely). However, guests generally favor this animated ride.

· **Magic Tips** ·
Easily check wait times on the free Universal Hollywood mobile app available for Apple and Android devices. We recommend downloading this ahead of your visit to prevent slow installation.

DESPICABLE ME: MINION MAYHEM

Ride with Gru, his kids, and of course, dozens of yellow minions in this motion simulator.

Ride Type: Motion simulation

Level: Young Kids, Kids, Tweens, Families

Height Restriction: 40" (102cm). Children must be at least 48" (122cm) to ride without an adult.

Recommendation: Perfect for families and fans of the *Despicable Me* films. While we find this ride to be adorable and a lot of fun, Thrill Riders may want to skip it.

SILLY SWIRLY FUN RIDE

A classic spinner ride (similar to Dumbo at the Disney theme parks) styled after characters in *Despicable Me*. Riders control the height of the ride with an easy-to-use joystick as it spins around this colorful mini land.

Ride Type: Spinner ride

Level: Young Kids, Kids

Height Restriction: Children must be at least 48" (121.9cm) to ride without an adult.

Recommendation: A spinning ride perfect for young kids.

SUPER SILLY FUN LAND

A water "soak zone" playground. Minions pose around this area for photo ops and other fun.

Ride Type: Water playground

Level: Young Kids, Kids

Height Restriction: Children must be 48" (121.9cm) or shorter to play.

Recommendation: A mini water park intended for young kids. Be sure to bring a change of clothes—they're going to get soaked!

⋆ Magic Tips ⋆
During cooler months (often January through March), Universal may close Super Silly Fun Land.

WATERWORLD

An explosive stunt show on the water starring characters and themes from the film *WaterWorld*. The explosions and stunts are fantastic and really like nothing you'll see anywhere else.

Show Length: 20 minutes

Recommendation: WaterWorld is a smash hit for nearly every visitor of Universal Studios Hollywood. Overall, the effects and action are family friendly, but real fire and stunts are used throughout the show. The closer you sit to the water, the better chances you have of getting wet. To stay dry, keep out of the labeled "soak zones."

Note: This attraction sometimes uses a Virtual Queue.

THE WIZARDING WORLD OF HARRY POTTER

Read about the Wizarding World of Harry Potter rides, shows, and other attractions in the next chapter.

LOWER LOT

TRANSFORMERS: THE RIDE-3D

Help the Autobots keep the Allspark away from the deadly Decepticons in this explosive 3D motion simulation ride.

Ride Type: Motion simulation with a moving vehicle

Level: Kids, Teens, Adults, Thrill Riders

Height Restriction: 40" (102cm). Children must be at least 48" (122cm) to ride without an adult.

Recommendation: Transformers is a well-told thrill ride with plenty of amazing action sequences. You'll really feel immersed in the film series as you battle massive enemy robots. If you're not familiar with the films, you may have a hard time following the storyline. However, Transformers is still a lot of fun and something that visitors of all ages can enjoy.

⋆ **Magic Tips** ⋆

Meet Optimus Prime, Bumblebee, and Megatron outside of this ride. The characters rotate throughout the day and the lines can become quite long to meet them. The giant robots interact with guests and make for some great photos!

REVENGE OF THE MUMMY

Universal Studios Hollywood's only thrilling rollercoaster. Themed after *The Mummy* film franchise, special effects, lighting, and an incredible launch sequence bring this attraction together. The ride even goes backward at one point!

Ride Type: Indoor rollercoaster

Level: Thrill Riders

Height Restriction: 40" (101.6cm). Children must be at least 48" (121.9cm) to ride without an adult.

Recommendation: A high-speed roller coaster that lags a bit at the end, but has some pretty cool special effects. Thrill riders will appreciate this indoor coaster.

JURASSIC WORLD—THE RIDE

A boat ride through the exhibits of Jurassic World! See dinosaurs brought to life before facing off against the terrifying Indominus Rex.

Ride Type: Boat flume ride

Level: Kids, Teens, Adults, Thrill Riders

Height Restriction: 42" (107cm). Children must be at least 48" (122cm) to ride without an adult.

Recommendation: Jurassic World starts off gentle, but ends with an 80-foot drop! Prepare to get wet on this thrilling water ride!

· Magic Tips ·

If you want to avoid getting soaked, sit in the back rows. The first three rows get the wettest!

RAPTOR ENCOUNTER

Blue the Velociraptor and Juliet the Triceratops greet guests just outside of Jurassic World – The Ride. While these are just costumed characters, their details are amazing and look great in photos. Blue is also a bit terrifying and could scare young kids. Universal Team Members are happy to snap photos of you with these dinosaurs using your phone camera.

⋆ **Magic Tips** ⋆

The Jurassic World DinoPlay area is a playground next to Jurassic World – The Ride and is designed for Young Kids. With dino-themed slides, bridges, and even a bone dig site, there's plenty for kids to do. DinoPlay also features shaded seating for parents and misters for hot days.

SUPER NINTENDO WORLD

Read about the Super Nintendo World rides, shows, and other attractions in a later chapter.

SINGLE RIDER

If a party has an odd number of guests, an empty seat may become available on a ride. To get the most guests on the attraction as possible, the Single Rider queue was invented. Many guests use the Single Rider line because it often moves much faster than a standard line. The trade-off is that guests ride alone rather than with their party. However, only a handful of attractions have a Single Rider line.

ATTRACTIONS WITH SINGLE RIDER

- Harry Potter and the Forbidden Journey
- Flight of the Hippogriff
- Jurassic World – The Ride
- Mario Kart: Bower's Challenge
- Revenge of the Mummy
- Transformers: The Ride – 3D

⋆ **Magic Tips** ⋆

Ultimately, we recommend the Single Rider line for teens and adults. Families with young kids should ride as a group because in many instances, minimum height requirements for riding without a guardian are enforced. We've listed these minimum requirements along with other height restrictions throughout this chapter.

CHAPTER FIVE

THE WIZARDING WORLD OF HARRY POTTER

INTRODUCTION

In May of 2007, Universal Orlando announced a new realm of themed entertainment for its guests. The Wizarding World would take visitors into the magical adventures of the *Harry Potter* films. There, they'd fly through Hogwarts Castle, shop in hotspots around Hogsmeade Village, and even drink the famous Butterbeer!

After opening in June of 2010 in Orlando, the Wizarding World of Harry Potter has entertained eager Harry Potter fans from around the world. There are rides, thrills, and seemingly real magic for all to enjoy! Best of all, the land feels totally real. It's like stepping into the *Harry Potter* series while living out your own unforgettable adventure.

Author J. K. Rowling is one of the creative forces behind Hogsmeade and helped to make this *Harry Potter*-themed land feel authentic. A visit to the Wizarding World is difficult to describe. There are sights, smells, and sounds for every sense. The snow-covered rooftops of Hogsmeade Village are stunning and the sight of Hogwarts Castle is jaw dropping. Even the actors from the films make appearances within the main ride, Harry Potter and the Forbidden Journey.

After the success of Orlando's expansion, Universal announced a Wizarding World for its Hollywood theme park in 2011. A near clone of the original version, Hollywood's would offer the Forbidden Journey ride, the Flight of the Hippogriff junior roller coaster, and plenty of shopping. In 2016, the Wizarding World of Harry Potter debuted at Universal Studios Hollywood. The launch came with record ticket sales and is one of Universal's most popular attractions.

In this chapter, we review the rides, shows, and shops found in the Wizarding World of Harry Potter. We give tips for venturing into this unique land to choose your own Harry Potter adventure. Build a wand, practice magic, and sample treats found in the many stores. The Wizarding World is like visiting a theme park within another theme park—and truly, there's nothing else like it!

RIDES

HARRY POTTER AND THE FORBIDDEN JOURNEY

A dark ride starring the characters of the *Harry Potter* films. Enter the magnificent Hogwarts castle and meet Harry Potter characters in the various rooms. Look for enchanted portraits, magic spells, a winding garden, and stunning artwork. The queue is just as entertaining as the ride. Once you board a specialized crane-like vehicle, you'll fly through Hogwarts to encounter a game of Quidditch, a runaway dragon, spitting spiders, and even soul-sucking Dementors. Harry Potter and the Forbidden Journey is one of the most unique rides in the world, and not to be missed!

Ride Type: Simulation ride with a moving vehicle

Level: Kids, Tweens, Teens, and Adults

Height Restriction: 48" (122cm)

Recommendation: Harry Potter and the Forbidden Journey can make some guests prone to motion sickness feel very ill. The ride vehicle uses a KUKA arm crane which leans back—almost upside down at some points. There are also several motion simulation parts in this ride that could affect riders with sensitivities. Guests with young children should note the "haunted house" style of this attraction. There are creeping spiders, scary Dementors, and several other terrifying features.

⋆ Magic Tips ⋆

If the line is too long, you may want to try the Single Rider line for this attraction. Ask a team member located near the line entrances if its a shorter wait for this line. Keep in mind that you likely won't ride with the rest of your party, but you could wait just a fraction of the time.

Due to the mechanics of this attraction, guests cannot bring bags or loose items such as sunglasses onto the ride. Free lockers are available near the start of the attraction's indoor queue. However, these lockers aren't very big and may not hold larger bags such as backpacks. For this, you may need to pay for a larger locker, starting around $10 for the day.

For those worried about the comfort of the ride vehicle, a test seat is available before entering the queue.

FLIGHT OF THE HIPPOGRIFF

An outdoor junior roller coaster located near Hogwarts Castle. A hippogriff is half eagle, half horse, and very moody. Hagrid, the groundskeeper at Hogwarts castle, once cared for a hippogriff named Buckbeak who befriends Harry Potter. This ride is inspired by that creature.

Type: Junior Rollercoaster

Level: Young Kids, Kids, Tweens

Height Restriction: 40" (102cm). Children must be at least 48" (122cm) to ride without an adult.

Recommendation: Flight of the Hippogriff is a great introductory roller coaster for kids who need a stepping stone to the bigger coasters. Though the ride is just over a minute in length, the track is smooth and fun for the whole family.

Note: The seats on this ride are designed for kids, so taller and larger guests may not sit comfortably in them.

SHOWS

OLLIVANDERS

Description: An intimate, 7-minute show where the wand chooses the wizard!

Review: Located next to the famous Ollivanders—where Harry Potter gets his wand—this show isn't to be missed by any Wizarding World fan. Garrick Ollivander, or one of his assistants, invites a lucky park guest to take part in the wand selection experience.

Only around 24 guests see the show at a time, so the line can get quite long for the brief experience. Still, we think that Ollivanders is one of the better shows at Universal for its magical and emotional storytelling sure to touch the hearts of all that experience it. Sadly, only one person per group gets chosen for a wand experience and keeping the wand costs full price (around $60).

⋆ Magic Tips ⋆

There isn't a surefire way to be chosen by Ollivander, but from what we've noticed, participants that are usually near the front and to his right get picked the most. Though there are always exceptions, he mostly chooses guests who appear between ages 8-20.

THE NIGHTTIME LIGHTS AT HOGWARTS CASTLE

One of the best shows at Universal Studios Hollywood is projected onto the Hogwarts Castle on select summer nights. This brief, 5-minute show runs about every 20 minutes in front of the castle.

THE DARK ARTS AT HOGWARTS CASTLE

Similar to the Nighttime Lights at Hogwarts Castle, this seasonal projection show covers the dark side of the Wizarding World. Projections display wicked curses, creatures, and even fantastic magic brought to life in mind-blowing ways!

⋆ Magic Tips ⋆

Viewing the Nighttime Lights or The Dark Arts at Hogwarts Castle may be difficult due to limited space. We recommend getting a times guide when you enter the park (near the maps) and arriving 20 minutes before showtime.

The best viewing spots are near Flight of the Hippogriff or the small stage where the Frog Choir and Triwizard Spirit Rally perform.

THE FROG CHOIR

See Hogwarts students and their singing toads perform songs from the Wizarding World. The singers are talented and the show runs about 10 minutes.

TRIWIZARD SPIRIT RALLY

See wizard students from foreign wizarding schools Durmstrang and Beauxbatons show their school spirit with dazzling choreographed routines. The show runs about 5 minutes and is a lot of fun to watch while sipping on Butterbeer.

WAND SPOTS

Wands purchased at Ollivanders come with a map of the various magic practice locations around Hogsmeade Village. In these spots, guests can test spells by moving their wand in specific directions. These movements trigger several magical happenings around Hogsmeade Village.

Using the wand magic can be a little tricky. However, team members are happy to assist. Look for team members standing around Hogsmeade Village, and they may instruct you on how to use your wand! After a couple of tries, it's easy to get the motions. Sometimes, you have to find the censor and perform exaggerated motions to get the "magic" to work.

DINING

Food is one of the best parts of the *Harry Potter* book series, and the Wizarding World is no different! We recommend trying some of the delicious sweets and eats around the lands—you might find something that amazes you.

THREE BROOMSTICKS

Dine in Hogsmeade Village's traditional eatery with British dishes and snacks. The Three Broomsticks is our favorite quick-service dining spot in Universal Studios Hollywood for its delicious food, themed dining, and large portions.

Type: Quick-Service (Lunch and Dinner)
Price: $$
Reservations: No
Menu Items: fish and chips, Cornish pasties, spare ribs, chicken, turkey leg, salads, shepherd's pie, Butterbeer, *Harry Potter*-themed desserts

THREE BROOMSTICKS RECOMMENDATIONS

Fish and Chips (entree) - Battered and fried fish served with thick-cut french fries and tartar sauce.

Spare Ribs Platter (entree) - Tangy barbecue pork ribs served with husked corn and roasted potatoes.

Shephard's Pie with Garden Salad (entree) - Flaky meat pie with beef, lamb, cooked veggies, and topped with mashed potatoes—served with a garden salad and choice of dressing.

Butterbeer Potted Cream (dessert) - Smooth butterscotch-flavored pudding with a dollop of whipped cream.

· Magic Tips ·
If you're planning on lunch at the Three Broomsticks on a busy day, we recommend getting there by 11:30am to avoid the lunch rush. For later lunching, head there after 2:30pm. Dinner at Three Broomsticks isn't as popular as midday dining.

MAGIC NEEP CART

Grab a bottle of Pumpkin Juice, Gillywater (regular bottled water), or beer in this *Harry Potter*-themed snack cart. The Magic Neep also sells fresh fruit and certain snacks. The line here is usually shorter than the spots around Hogsmeade Village.

HOG'S HEAD

Located in the back of the Three Broomsticks restaurant, the Hog's Head is a famous Wizarding World pub from the books and film. There are delicious drinks here for guests of all ages and alcoholic beverages for those over 21. The bartenders are usually very friendly and can help you decide which drink to purchase. Behind the bar is a moving hog head that's magically brought to life!

Type: Bar
Price: $-$$
Reservations: No
Drinks: Butterbeer (soda, frozen, and hot), Pumpkin Juice, Gillywater, mixed drinks, beers, wine

HOG'S HEAD RECOMMENDATIONS

Dragonscale Ale (alcoholic beverage) - An amber lager with caramel malt flavors.

Pear Dazzle (alcoholic beverage) - A fruity mixed drink with vodka, pear cider, lemonade, and a cherry on top!

Hog's Head Brew (alcoholic beverage) - A mild, smooth red ale with a small "hop" and tangy taste.

Fishy Green Ale (nonalcoholic beverage) - A mint and cinnamon drink with tart blueberry-flavored "fish egg" popping pearls.

Tongue Tying Lemon Squash (nonalcoholic beverage) - A refreshing lemonade with a fresh-squeezed and lightly sweet taste.

Peachtree Fizzing Tea (nonalcoholic beverage) - A lightly sweet iced tea with peach and ginger flavors.

⋆ **Magic Tips** ⋆
The Hog's Head Brew is a popular beer only served at the Hog's Head in Hogsmeade Village!

There's a secret menu item served at the Hog's Head called The Triple—or the Deathly Hallows. It's an alcoholic drink with cider, Hog's Head Brew, and Guinness. It's a nice treat for beer lovers looking for some extra adventure in their drink!

THE BEST SNACKS AND DRINKS

BUTTERBEER – A delicious, non-alcoholic butterscotch soda served with a whipped cream topping. Butterbeer comes as a traditional soda or a less sweet frozen (slushy) version. Find it at the Butterbeer Carts around Hogsmeade Village, Hog's Head, and Three Broomsticks. Butterbeer also comes in a "hot" form which is served sort of like a rich and creamy latte.

⋆ **Magic Tips** ⋆
Three Broomsticks also serves a vegan version of Butterbeer that tastes very similar to the original!

We love mixing the Hog's Head Brew (beer) with Butterbeer (if you're 21 years or older). It's not for everyone, but if you enjoy sweeter beers, this makes for a great combination! You'll have to order them separately and try them together.

CHOCOLATE FROG - A deliciously creamy, solid milk chocolate frog. Each frog comes with a holographic collectable card featuring a famous wizard! Get these at Honeydukes. Makes a great gift to take home!

BUTTERBEER FUDGE - An ultra-sweet bar of creamy butterscotch flavor. Get this treat at Honeydukes in Hogsmeade Village.

NO-MELT ICE CREAM - Served like traditional ice cream in a variety of flavors—like chocolate, vanilla, and even pumpkin—this delicious treat isn't ice cream at all. Instead, it's similar to whipped cream which means that it won't melt even on the hottest day. Find it at Honeydukes in Hogsmeade Village.

PUMPKIN PASTIES - A flaky, pumpkin pie-flavored pastry. Pumpkin Pasties can be purchased at Honeydukes in Hogsmeade Village.

PUMPKIN JUICE - This nonalcoholic drink comes in a very cool bottle with a pumpkin-shaped cap. The flavor is a swirl of apple juice, pumpkin puree, sugar, and other fruity flavors. It seems that there's a dash of nutmeg and other spices that make this cold, sweet drink taste like a Christmas beverage. We highly recommend trying Pumpkin Juice, especially for those with a sweet tooth. Get it at carts around Hogsmeade Village.

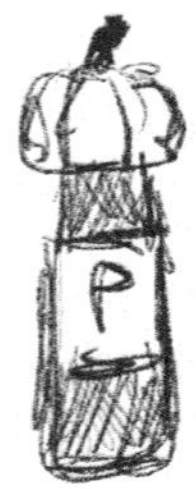

Note: Many of the snack carts sell bottles of Gillywater. While this drink looks interesting, it's nothing more than typical bottled water with a fancy, *Harry Potter*-themed label (in the books and films, the similarly named gillyweed gave Harry Potter the ability to breath underwater).

SHOPPING

DERVISH AND BANGES

Think of this store as the gift shop of Hogsmeade Village. Get everything from t-shirts to broomsticks here to take home! Dervish and Banges is also a great spot for getting Hogwarts House-related items like Gryffindor and Slytherin goods. All of the merchandise is beautifully crafted to appease even the most scrutinizing Harry Potter fan. Of course, this also means that the prices are fairly high for some of the goods. We recommend setting aside a budget before visiting.

· Magic Tips ·

Everything in Dervish and Banges—as well as the rest of the Wizarding World of Harry Potter—is designed to appear authentic to the story. This means that you'll be able to find merchandise and apparel that Harry Potter could have purchased himself. For that reason, you won't find a t-shirt that reads "The Wizarding World of Harry Potter" here. For those, you'll need to purchase at stores outside of the Wizarding World.

Have you ever been sorted into a Harry Potter house? If not, we recommend visiting **WizardingWorld.com**, the official website for all things Harry Potter. Sign up for a free account to discover your Hogwarts House and other magical designations. Then, once you arrive in Hogsmeade Village, you'll know which of the schools you belong to for merchandise purchases!

OWL POST

Take home an owl stuffed animal or mail parcels and letters to loved ones from this unique location. Friends and family love receiving packages stamped with the Hogsmeade seal.

FILCH'S EMPORIUM OF CONFISCATED GOODS

Get school supplies based on the houses of Hogwarts and more. There are also toys, robes, and even cases filled with neat Harry Potter artifacts that aren't for sale—including a Marauder's Map with footsteps moving about the paper!

HONEYDUKES

Pick out your choice of sweet on seemingly endless shelves of candy. We recommend checking out the baked goods counter for some extra-delicious dessert options.

ZONKO'S JOKE SHOP

This toy store sells colorful wizarding gifts and goods. Find Harry Potter-themed favorites here like an Extendable Ear (listening device) or a Pygmy Puff, an adorable plush toy to take home. Enter Zonko's Joke Shop through Honeydukes.

MORE SHOPS

Wiseacre's Wizarding Equipment and Gladrags Wizardwear sell robes and other accessories from the Harry Potter universe. Guests can try on robes before purchasing to ensure that the fit is just right!

SECRETS OF HOGSMEADE VILLAGE

He-Who-Must-Not-Be-Named – Some of the team members working in the Wizarding World do not enjoy hearing Voldemort's name. Have a little fun with them and mention him to see what they say!

A Familiar Voice – In the restrooms, listen for the voice of Moaning Myrtle as she giggles in the pipes!

Free Elf – In the Three Broomsticks, look near the ceiling for Dobby's shadow! He seems to be practicing magic for a certain wizard boy.

Cool Witchcraft – In the queue for Harry Potter and the Forbidden Journey, stick around in the Dark Arts room to see Hermione magically pour snow all over the room!

Dropping By – Look up toward the ceiling in the Owl Post and you'll see the birds hooting above. Look down and you'll see their mess, so watch your step!

You're in Trouble Now! – When a wizard or witch has misbehaved, they might receive an angry-voiced letter called a Howler. Outside the Owl Post, you can see a Howler appear on a certain spot to scream at you!

Cuckowl Clock – Every now and then you'll see an owl pop out of a small door atop the Owlery!

Little Headed – To the left of the hog's head (in its pub), look for three shrunken heads. These are from the movie *Harry Potter and the Prisoner of Azkaban*!

More in Store – Harry Potter fanatics may want to explore Hogsmeade for additional storefronts. There are several windows to stores (that cannot be entered) including Madam Puddifoot's Teas & Cakes!

The Mirror of Erised – Blink and you might miss this Harry Potter throwback! Once inside Hogswarts Castle, you could easily walk past one of the series' most iconic items. The Mirror of Erised sits, covered in cobwebs, in the hallway before heading to the garden.

WIZARDING WORLD CHRISTMAS

During the holiday season, the Wizarding World transforms with Christmas magic. See wreaths and other decorations adorning Hogsmeade Village. On select nights (usually around the weekends and holiday weeks), Hogwarts Castle has a special display of The Magic of Christmas, a projection show. This beautiful nighttime event is worth seeing and runs about every 20 minutes.

Special holiday snacks and sweets are found during this season in various shops. You can also try Hot Butterbeer in Three Broomsticks! The Frog Choir in Hogsmeade Village performs holiday songs daily. The holiday celebrations run from mid-November through the first week of January.

⋆ Magic Tips ⋆

The nighttime shows can become packed and team members may not allow you near the castle until after the show. The show concludes with fireworks, so once you spot these, head over for the next showing as the crowd clears.

CHAPTER SIX

SUPER NINTENDO WORLD

INTRODUCTION

Immersive theme park experiences have just leveled up! With Super Nintendo World, Universal Studios Hollywood created a video game-based playground for all ages. Based on the Mushroom Kingdom from Nintendo's Super Mario Bros. franchise, these explorable areas are filled with interactive features, boss battles, a shop, an immersive ride, and Universal's best quick-service dining spot.

Super Nintendo World's footprint isn't very big but it makes up for its size with physical levels. Guests can collect coins and explore areas on different floors. The lower floor is the entry way with toadstool seats, boss battles, and entrances to the ride, shopping, and dining. Stairs climb up to the upper level where guests can explore icy caves and even stargaze with augmented reality telescopes.

Rather than a traditional themed land filled with rides, Nintendo wanted more interactive elements. Similar to its gaming consoles, Nintendo invites fans to experience new ways to play together—and Super Nintendo World delivers exciting gameplay for those willing to participate!

GETTING INTO THE GAME

Immersive elements around Super Nintendo World allow guests to play and unlock new activities. Using the Universal Studios Hollywood app, guests can log into the Super Nintendo World section to find a map of the land, activity locations, dining, and more. If you'd like to familiarize yourself with the land before visiting, we recommend opening the app as you review this part of the chapter.

Question mark boxes around the land allow guests to tap the base of them to collect coins. You shouldn't hit the boxes too hard but after a nice tap of your hand, you can hear sounds. If successful, you'll hear a ringing noise that means you've collected a coin. Other sounds could

mean that the box is empty and that you should return later. Some boxes allow you to tap out more coins than others.

Universal Studios sells a Power-Up Band that allows you to keep track of the coins you've collected. These wearable wrist straps are designed after several characters including Mario, Luigi, Princess Peach, Toad, Yoshi, and Princess Daisy. At about $40 each, these bands sync to your Universal Studios Hollywood app and register your achievements. The coins you collect will also tally together in digital scoreboards for the entire land. The character you choose allows you to join a team like Mario, Peach, Toad, etc. and the coins you collect will help your team's overall score. However, digital coins are not exchangeable for physical items. Instead, they are used just for competitive gameplay. Power-Up Bands can be purchased at many retail locations inside Universal Studios Hollywood including the 1-Up Store and vending machines within Super Nintendo World. However, guests can also purchase in other retail locations parkwide before entering the land.

The Power-Up Bands also allow guests to collect digital key coins within Super Nintendo World. Key coins are earned in four different boss battles found within the land. Guests perform simple but fun tasks to defeat bosses like quickly cranking a lever to topple a goomba. Once you've collected 3 key coins, you can head over to Bower Jr.'s lair and battle him. Bowser Jr.'s boss battle is by far the most entertaining interactive game within the land. Guests team up to collect power ups like fireballs and defeat the boss!

RIDES

MARIO KART: BOWSER'S CHALLENGE

There is one ride-through attraction in Super Nintendo World and it's based on the Mario Kart video game series. Guests ride together through massive scenes and wear augmented reality headsets shaped like Mario's signature red cap. The AR technology brings to life digital characters that race through physical sets. However, guests are not racing each other, rather they are to outpace the villain Bowser and his many minions. Rather than a fast-paced rather (the karts move rather slowly) guests can pick up and toss digital koopa shells at enemies. Successfully hitting targets gifts the guest digital coins. The goal is to collect 100 coins to unlock a the highest honor, Universal's virtual trophy cup. If you're using the Power-Up band you'll be able to tap it the "M" of your steering wheel and collect the coins earned during the ride.

Ride Type: Simulation ride with a moving vehicle

Level: Kids, Tweens, Teens, and Adults

Height Restriction: 40" (102cm)

Recommendation: Mario Kart: Bowser's Challenge is an attraction is great for those who live interactive gameplay within rides. The queue to this ride has some impressive set pieces including Yoshi's Island and Bower's fortress! Guests collect and shoot koopa shells, aiming with their headset and firing with a steering wheel. So you'll see both physical set pieces and digital characters racing around your during the ride. We find that this attraction is more fun with each ride through. However, lines can get very long, so we recommend visiting early in the day and riding it first.

· Magic Tips ·

Universal Studios gives a disclaimer that guests with waist sizes over 40" may not fit inside the vehicle. Though many guests with waist sizes larger than 40" have reported no problem riding, Universal has a test seat available at the entrance of the ride. It's tucked around a corner so out of site from most guests in line.

Scoring Tips:

The ultimate goal is to collect 100 coins during the ride and unlock the Universal trophy! Here's what we recommend for getting the most coins:

1. **Turning** – You can collect coins by successfully turning your steering wheel! Once you see arrows in your AR headset, turn your wheel in that direction. Some turns require more steering so in this instance, the arrows may light up red! It's a bit tricky to navigate steering and tossing koopa shells but don't ignore the steering!
2. **Practice** – The first part of the ride allows you to practice aiming and shooting turtle shells. Use this time to learn the best aim methods!
3. **Aim Right** – You'll also want to watch where you aim because hitting a character like Mario will lose coins. However, hitting a digital foe will gain you coins!
4. **Watch the Number** – You have a limited number of koopa shells, so be careful not to shoot them all at the beginning. Your AR headset displays the number of remaining shells. Your kart will pass through question blocks that refill your shells throughout the ride.

· Magic Tips ·
Similar to the Mario Kart video games, guests can get a head start during the countdown of the race. You'll hear a "3...2...1..." announcement and if you press both trigger buttons at the same time right before "2" you'll earn bonus coins!

INTERACTIVE EXPERIENCES

BOWSER JUNIOR SHADOW SHOWDOWN

If you have a Power-Up Band, you can take on four different bad guys within Super Nintendo World and unlock the Bowser Junior boss battle. Really, you only need to defeat three of the four baddies but they are (you don't need a Power-Up Band to play these attractions, only to collect key coins):

- ✦ **Goomba Crazy Crank** – A mini game where guests crank a lever as fast as they can to topple a goomba!
- ✦ **Piranha Plant Nap Mishap** – Joining with other players, guests race around a small area smashing buzzing clocks.
- ✦ **Thwomp Panel Panic** – Enter a cave and turn over as many blocks you can within a limited time!
- ✦ **Koopa Troopa POWer Punch** – Get the timing right and smash a block to start a chain reaction that defeats a koopa!

Once you've collected enough coins, head to Bower Jr.'s lair to the left of the Mario Kart ride entrance. Show the Team Member your phone with the three key coins to enter! The boss battle walks you through a story where Bowser Jr. has stolen a golden mushroom. It's up to you and about 10 other players to batter him and take back the prized mushroom. During the game, your shadow is projected onto a digital wall where you can swat bombs at him and collect power-ups like mushrooms and fire flowers!

· Magic Tips ·
If you don't have a Power-Up Band but still want to play the Bower Junior Shadow Showdown, it's worth asking a Team Member at the attraction entrance. You're not guaranteed to enter but still worth asking!

CHARACTERS

Mario and Luigi greet guests in the center of Super Nintendo World. Princess Peach poses for pictures in her gazebo near the entrance to the land. You can also meet Toad! To avoid lines, we recommend lining up before they get to their spot. Showtimes are often posted outside of the queue for these characters. If you have the Power-Up Band, you'll unlock stamps within the app for meeting all of the characters.

DINING

There are two different food locations themed for Super Nintendo World. The main dining hall is Toadstool Cafe where guests can try burgers, pasta, and more themed after Super Mario characters. This indoor restaurant is round like a giant mushroom cap and there are several tables and booths to dine. Around the walls are digital screens showing toadstools running around the restaurant.

We recommend the Luigi Pesto Chicken Burger and the ? Block Tiramisu. Unfortunately, there aren't reservations for the Toadstool Cafe (unless Universal changes this later), so guests must put their name in at the entrance of the restaurant.

The second snack spot is located just outside Super Nintendo World near the entrance to Jurassic World the Ride. Super Snacks serves popcorn and flavored cream sodas. These tasty fruit-flavored sodas have whipped toppings and popping boba. Guests can also pick up Mario-themed popcorn buckets here!

TOADSTOOL CAFE RECOMMENDATIONS

Luigi Burger Pesto Grilled Chicken (entree) - A grilled chicken sandwich on a brioche bun with with basil pesto, Swiss cheese, a thick green pepper, and spinach. It's served with a side of truffle French fries and garnished with a Luigi cap toothpick!

Chef Toad Short Rib Special (entree) - A pile of braised short rib, goat cheese polenta, mushrooms, red wine reduction, and topped with a Chef Toad Parmesan cracker.

? Block Tiramisu (dessert) - Several question-mark square cookies around a creaming tiramisu center! We hardly taste the coffee in this one!

Super Star Lemon Squash (drink) - Honey lemon soda with mango star jellies and tropical popping boba

⋆ Magic Tips ⋆
On busier days, getting a table at Cafe Toadstool can be tricky! We recommend heading to the restaurant earlier in the day to put your name in. You may be asked to wait or to get a text when your table is ready. If the cafe is full, there may not be a waiting list available.

SNACK CART

Outside of Super Nintendo World, in the Lower Lot, guests can try themed drinks and popcorn. Our guess is that there wasn't enough room inside Super Nintendo World for this snack cart so they opted to place this cart near the entrance of Jurassic World The Ride. It's also good news for fans wanting to try Mario-themed snacks before entering the land. Here you can try Fruity Cream Sodas and popcorn. There are also collectable sippers and popcorn holders. We recommend the Princess Peach's Peach Soda or Mario's Strawberry Soda!

SHOPPING

1-UP FACTORY

The 1-Up Factory is the central store in Super Nintendo World. Guests can find Mario Bros.-themed apparel, gifts, Power-Up Bands, and more within this store. It's also the exit shop for the Mario Kart ride.

NINTENDO WORLD SECRETS

8-Bit Characters – There are four hidden 8-bit Mario characters hidden throughout Super Nintendo World. You can find their locations within the Universal Studios Hollywood app, in the Super Nintendo World map. Just tap your Power-Up Band on the hidden "M" to active them. Collecting them all earns coins and stamps within the app!

Toadstool Attack! – During your dining experience inside the Toadstool Cafe, look at the digital windows. You may see them running around or even hiding as Bowser attacks!

Spotting Pikmin – Several characters from Nintendo's Pikmin series can be spotted around Super Nintendo World!

Galactic Friends – The AR binoculars on the second level of Super Nintendo World can be used to see new features around the land. However, if you zoom into the sky, you can spot a Super Mario Galaxy nod—Rosalina in her Comet Observatory!

Power Amiibo – At home, you can use your Power-Up Band with your Nintendo Switch! Certain games will allow you to tap it as you would an Amiibo and unlock power-ups. Try it with Mario Kart 8!

VISITING TIPS

Super Nintendo World has been incredibly popular since it first debuted in early 2023. We don't expect demand for this new land to slow in 2024. During busy days, Universal may implement the Virtual Line to enter the land. You can join this queue once you've entered Universal Studios via the app. Sometimes you can join the queue in the parking structure or CityWalk. Once your time in called, you'll get a notification on the app to visit the land. Guests may stay as long as they'd like inside Super Nintendo World and other guests are allowed inside once others leave.

Guests who arrive early to the park may not have to use the virtual queue. So we recommend getting to the park before open to be the first inside. Even if you wait for your virtual queue time, you still may find yourself inside a crowded land. This could mean 30-minute waits for the interactive games as well and possibly a 2-hour wait for Mario Kart: Bower's Challenge. In addition, you may find that the Toadstool Cafe has reached capacity and you won't be able to dine there.

The best way to avoid crowds, even on the busiest days, is it purchase Earl Entry for Super Nintendo World. Sold on UniversalStudios.com, this pass allows guests to enter the land one hour before park opening. Prices start at $20 per person, per day and work as an addition to your ticket (you must have valid theme park admission for early entry). We recommend riding Mario Kart first and then the interactive games before heading to the Toadstool Cafe, should you be in the mood for eating. Usually crowds are kept lower enough to allow for all of this within the first hour.

CHAPTER SEVEN

UNIVERSAL CITYWALK

INTRODUCTION

The Universal CityWalk is a mall meets entertainment hotspot. Guests do not need theme park admission to enter this shopping district. During the day, CityWalk is home to a collection of specialty shops, themed restaurants, and snack spots. At night, neon lights illuminate the area, bringing a lively, almost Vegas-like feel. However, unlike Las Vegas, CityWalk is small and packed together. The dozens of shops and restaurants layer on top of one another, inviting guests to explore all that it has to offer.

PARKING

Parking works the same for CityWalk as it does Universal Studios Hollywood. However, shopping or dining at CityWalk can score you limited parking validation—usually for 2 hours.

ENTERTAINMENT

UNIVERSAL CINEMA

See a newly released movie or experience the stunning visuals of IMAX in this 19-screen movie theater. The theater has reclining seats, a full bar, and a slylish concession stand.

⋆ Magic Tips ⋆

Get $5 parking when you purchase a ticket here. The parking is good for all day!

AMC Stubs members can get a $5 movie ticket and discounted concessions on select weekdays. Sign up for a free Stubs membership at AMCTheatres.com.

5 TOWERS STAGE

An outdoor concert venue for local and cover bands. A 5,000 LED light backdrop sets the stage for this unique venue!

iFLY

Take flight in this wind tunnel designed to simulate skydiving! While there's a bit of a learning curve, iFly invites guests ages 3 and older to try out this amazing experience. For more information and booking, visit their official website: https://www.iflyworld.com/hollywood.

⋆ Magic Tips ⋆

At about $60 per person, iFly can be a little pricey. However, weekdays and advanced tickets tend to be cheaper.

ACCESS HOLLYWOOD

See live tapings of the entertainment show right by the famous Universal Studios rotating globe! You may even spot Mario Lopez and other stars! Filming times vary, but they tend to occur midweek.

FEATURED SHOPS

Like many American malls, the shops at CityWalk change from year to year. We've highlighted some of the more unique spots to shop during your visit:

Abercrombie & Fitch – Casual clothing and accessories

Hot Topic – Music and pop culture apparel and accessories

IT'SUGAR – A gift shop with plenty of treats, pleasant smells, and more

LIDS – Custom sport and casual hats

The Los Angeles Sock Market – Choose from hundreds of sock designs in this unique shop.

Tillys – Beach and sport-inspired clothing and accessories

Universal Studios Store – Clothing and gifts inspired by Universal Studios. Get everything from Marvel to Harry Potter in this unique shop.

Note: We detail Universal CityWalk's best restaurants in the next chapter.

CHAPTER EIGHT

DINING GUIDE

INTRODUCTION

Just as it themes attractions, Universal Studios Hollywood also themes its food. From a Simpsons-style courtyard to authentic British favorites in the Wizarding World of Harry Potter, there's much to sample around the park.

Some of our favorite theme park snacks are only found at Universal, like the Big Pink donut served at Lard Lad Donuts. The dining in Hogsmeade Village is also spectacular with plenty of fun treats to take home or enjoy on-site.

Most of the dining spots in the theme park are "quick service" or to-go counters. While there is seating, you won't find a traditional waiter within the park. Instead, CityWalk offers plenty of table service experiences with a wide variety of dining choices. While many of the CityWalk restaurants are chains, others offer unique entertainment and other experiences.

Aside from CityWalk, a lot of the food at Universal Studios Hollywood isn't very remarkable. Most of the burgers, sandwiches, and other American favorites are very middle of the road (or worse).

To help you navigate through the good, the bad, and the ugly, we've detailed the many dining areas around the parks and highlighted our favorites!

RESTAURANT TYPES

Quick Service – Fast order meals where you often choose your own seating.

Table Service – Restaurants with a waiter. It is suggested that you tip based on the service you receive.

Snack Location – Small kiosks or dining windows with a smaller selection of food and drink.

Bars and Lounges – Areas with open seating and typically a full bar.

OUR RESTAURANT PRICING

Symbol	Price Range	Restaurant Type
$	Under $10	Typically Snack Carts
$$	$10 - $20	Typically Quick Service
$$$	$20 - $35	Table Service Restaurants
$$$$	$35	Fine or Themed Dining

LOOK FOR THE HEARTS

We also list our favorites from snacks to dining locations. Just look for the "❤" next to the item to see our most recommended places!

COCA-COLA FREESTYLE

If you plan on enjoying several soda drinks throughout the day, we recommend purchasing the Coca-Cola Freestyle Cup. This plastic drink cup comes with unlimited fountain drink refills throughout the day at participating locations within the theme park.

We enjoy the Coca-Cola Freestyle cup because you can choose from over 100 drink options including Coke, Diet Coke, and Sprite. There are also several variations of Coke products like vanilla and fruit flavors, if you so choose.

Furthermore, cold, filtered water is dispensed from these machines, so it's a much cheaper option than buying water bottles.

Most of the quick service dining locations offer Freestyle refills. However, to better stick with its central theming, the Wizarding World of Harry Potter does not have these machines.

Freestyle cups start at $17.00 each or two for $16.00 each. Cups no longer work in the machines at the end of the day.

RESTAURANTS WITH FREESTYLE

We've marked all of the dining spots offering the Coca-Cola Freestyle refills with the "**Ω**" symbol.

UPPER LOT DINING

HOLLYWOOD AND DINE Ω

Description: A Los Angeles-style café

Dining Type: Quick Service

Location: Near the entrance

Pricing: $$

Menu Overview: Burgers, sandwiches, pizza, Asian chicken bowl, vegan burger, chicken Caesar salad, fries, onion rings, desserts, soda, coffee, tea, juice, beer.

Review: Certainly not the best food in the park, but could satisfy someone looking for a quick burger. The outside theming looks fun, and has a very "Hollywood" appeal.

However, the inside is a stale ordering counter. Seating is located just outside of the restaurant.

Recommendation: Asian Chicken Bowl

❤ STARBUCKS

Description: Chain coffee shop

Dining Type: Snack Location

Location: Upper Lot, near the entrance

Pricing: $

Menu Overview: coffee, tea, and pastries

Review: Grab your favorite Starbucks drink just steps away from the theme park entrance.

> ⋆ **Magic Tips** ⋆
> Lines for Starbucks are crowded early in the morning. You may want to wait about 30 minutes after opening for the lines to die down.

MINION CAFE Ω

Description: Grilled Cheese Sandwiches and more

Dining Type: Quick Service

Location: Near Despicable Me: Minion Mayhem

Pricing: $$

Menu Overview: Grilled cheese sandwiches, mac n cheese, ramen bowl, nachos, chicken tenders, desserts, soda, coffee, chocolate milk, juice, beer.

Review: Kid-friendly meals with grilled cheese, fries, and more all themed to Minions from *Despicable Me*.

Recommendation: Classic Grilled Cheese (comes with fries and marinara dipping sauce)

COCINA MEXICANA Ω

Description: Fast Mexican food

Dining Type: Quick Service

Location: Near Universal Plaza (central hub)

Pricing: $$

Menu Overview: Tacos, burritos, salads, churros, soda, margaritas, beer.

Review: If you're craving Mexican food there are some pretty standard choices here. However, we enjoy Bumblebee Man's Tacos a bit more. Cocina Mexicana doesn't have its own seating. Instead, look for seats nearby or in the Duff Brewery Beer Garden.

Recommendation: Beef Nachos

PALACE DELI & MARKET Ω

Description: Grab-and-go sandwiches

Dining Type: Quick Service

Location: Near Universal Plaza (central hub)

Pricing: $-$$

Menu Overview: Sandwiches, salads, sushi, snacks, desserts, bottled water, tea, coffee, beer, wine.

Review: Find healthier, pre-made sandwiches and snack items here. Palace Deli doesn't have much seating, but is intended to satisfy guest cravings as they wander the theme park. For seating, go to the nearby Universal Plaza or Duff Brewery Beer Garden.

Recommendation: Turkey and Swiss Croissant Sandwich

MEL'S DINER Ω

Description: As featured in the George Lucas film *American Graffiti*, this 50s-style diner is a Hollywood staple.

Dining Type: Quick Service

Location: Near Universal Plaza (central hub)

Pricing: $$

Menu Overview: Sandwiches, salads, pastries, coffee, espresso, tea, soda, beer, wine.

Review: Though it's themed after the Mel's Diner found on Hollywood & Vine, the two locations are nothing alike. Universal's version has a limited menu of burgers, sandwiches, and salads. However, instead of a traditional side of fries, these entrees come with tater tots (pieces of crispy, fried potato). Mel's has plenty of seating inside the restaurant and outdoors. During the off-season, this dining spot only opens for lunch.

Recommendation: Fried Chicken Sandwich with tater tots

FRENCH STREET BISTRO

Description: Coffee and grab-and-go sandwiches

Dining Type: Quick Service

Location: Near Universal Plaza (central hub)

Pricing: $-$$

Menu Overview: Sandwiches, salads, pastries, coffee, espresso, tea, soda.

Review: Discover a wide variety of hot and cold brews in this quaint dining spot. There are only a few seats within the bistro, as it's made for those wishing to grab a drink or bite and walk around.

Recommendation: Turkey and Swiss Croissant Sandwich or Brownie of the Month

MORE EATS

CHURRO CARTS ($) – Snack on classic cinnamon and sugar-dusted fried sweets. Also try seasonal flavors like strawberry shortcake, toasted coconut, and double dark chocolate. We highly recommend asking the churro cart Team Member for a fresh one as they taste the best!

UNIVERSAL TOWER SNACK BAR ($) – Located near the theme park's entrance, this snack station is mostly known for its Jumbo Turkey Legs.

❤ **MULLIGAN'S IRISH PUB** ($) – Grab a beer-on-tap or a snack in this indoor bar. Seating is limited, and the bar may not be open on weekdays during the off-season. We recommend the Irish Mule, a mix of Irish whiskey, ginger beer, and lime.

· **Magic Tips** ·
Secret Drink Alert! Adults 21+, ask for the "Jurassic Water" at Mulligan's Irish Pub. It's a delicious mix of vodka, rum, tequila, blue curaçao, gin, and fruit liqueurs with soda!

❤ **DESPICABLE DELIGHTS** ($) – Try a smoothie or dessert cup in this *Despicable Me*-inspired snacking station. We recommend the Freeze Ray Smoothie with banana and mango flavors!

SPRINGFIELD, U.S.A.

❤ LARD LAD DONUTS

Description: *The Simpsons*-themed donuts and drinks

Dining Type: Snacking Station

Location: Springfield, U.S.A.

Pricing: $

Menu Overview: Donuts, coffee, tea, milk, soda.

Review: If you've ever wanted to try Homer Simpson's favorite donuts, head to Lard Lad near the entrance to Springfield, U.S.A. Universal serves both giant-sized and smaller versions of these treats along with coffee, tea, and bottled water.

Recommendation: The Big Pink – a giant, shareable donut with pink icing

· **Magic Tips** ·

If the line for Lard Lad's is too long, The Big Pink donut can also be found at the Kwik-E-Mart nearby.

KRUSTY BURGER Ω

Description: A spoof of McDonald's, this *Simpsons*-themed fast food restaurant serves American favorites.

Dining Type: Quick Service

Location: Springfield, U.S.A.

Pricing: $$

Menu Overview: Burgers, fries, salad, milk shake, soda, beer.

Review: In the world of The Simpsons, Krusty Burger is an unhealthy and, frankly, disgusting place. While Universal's version isn't disgusting, the food isn't remarkable. Expect standard burgers and fries with an excellent theme for fans of the animated TV series. There is plenty of indoor seating at Krusty Burger.

Recommendation: The Ribwich (a pork sandwich with barbecue sauce)

> **· Magic Tips ·**
> Dining spots around Springfield serve specialty beverages from the show. Buzz Cola is a take on Coca-Cola beverages and Duff Beer is similar to Budweiser.

❤ CLETUS' CHICKEN SHACK Ω

Description: Fried chicken fast food restaurant

Dining Type: Quick Service

Location: Springfield, U.S.A.

Pricing: $$

Menu Overview: Fried chicken, chicken sandwiches, fries, salad, milk shake, beer, soda.

Review: Fried chicken sandwiches have recently risen in popularity, and Cletus' Chicken Shack has its own notable version. The food is consistently better at Cletus' than Krusty Burger. Indoor seating here is shared with Krusty Burger.

Recommendation: Thrilled to be Grilled Chicken Sandwich

❤ BUMBLEBEE MAN'S TACOS

Description: Taco truck

Dining Type: Quick Service

Location: Springfield, U.S.A.

Pricing: $$

Menu Overview: Tacos, nachos, soda, beer.

Review: This food truck sells tacos, nachos, and beer. Seating is available in the Duff Brewery Beer Garden courtyard.

Recommendation: Bumblebee Man's Mucho Macho Nachos (with beef)

LUIGI'S PIZZA Ω

Description: Grab-and-go pizza slices

Dining Type: Quick Service

Location: Springfield, U.S.A.

Pricing: $$

Menu Overview: Pizza, pasta, beer, soda.

Review: Pizza here can be ordered by the slice. However, full pies are available upon request. Purchasing a full pie saves a few dollars and takes 10-15 minutes to cook. Seating is available in the Duff Brewery Beer Garden courtyard.

Recommendation: Meat Liker's Pizza (topped with sausage, pepperoni, meatballs, and bacon)

> ⋆ **Magic Tips** ⋆
>
> The humor in Springfield is everywhere, especially in the restaurants. Krusty Burger's slogan is "Over Dozens Sold" and Luigi's signature dish is the Fat Tony's Witness-Protected Pasta & Meatballs. While the food taste may not be outstanding, the details certainly leave an impression.

MORE SPRINGFIELD EATS

❤ **DUFF BREWERY** ($) – Homer Simpson's favorite beer is actually pretty tasty! In fact, we prefer it over other standard American beers. The flavor is pretty mild, but it's tastier than some of the watered-down beer flavors.

❤ **MOE'S TAVERN** ($) – Order a Duff Beer or try a non-alcoholic Flaming Moe (a smoking orange soda).

PHINEAS Q. BUTTERFAT'S ICE CREAM ($) – Try a cup of ice cream with your choice of flavor and toppings.

SUDS MCDUFF'S HOT DOGS ($) – Hot dogs and pretzels to go along with a Duff Beer.

HOGSMEADE VILLAGE

❤ While we've detailed Hogsmeade options in our previous chapter, the dining here is the best in the park. Our favorite, Three Broomsticks, has a variety of delicious entrees, sweets, and drinks that are fantastic.

· **Magic Tips** ·
During your day at Universal Studios, we recommend stopping by Hogsmeade Village at least twice. First, early in the morning to ride the attractions and then again for lunch or dinner at Three Broomsticks. Lunch crowds typically die down around 2PM on busier dates.

LOWER LOT DINING

❤ JURASSIC CAFE Ω

Description: A Costa Rica-inspired diner

Dining Type: Quick Service

Location: Near Jurassic World the Ride

Pricing: $$

Menu Overview: Chicken sandwich, chicken tenders, tuna poke bowl, salad, kids meals, desserts, soda, beer.

Review: The previous version of Jurassic Cafe was the worst dining spot in the entire park. However, after a recent revamp, the quick service eatery is now one of the best. With savory selections of chicken and pork, there's a wide variety of delicious menu options here. Jurassic Cafe also has plenty of indoor and outdoor seating.

Recommendation: Isla Chicken Sandwich or Slow Roasted Mojo Pork

---

❤ TOADSTOOL CAFE

Description: Super Mario-themed restaurant

Dining Type: Quick Service

Location: Inside Super Nintendo World

Pricing: $$

Menu Overview: Burgers, Italian food, salads, and desserts

Review: Easily the best restaurant inside Universal Studios Hollywood, the Toadstool Cafe is a fully-immersive dining experience. You'll see digital toadstools running around as you dine on delicious Italian and fusion burgers.

Recommendation: Luigi Chicken Burger (Pesto), Super Star Lemon Squash, ? Block Tiramisu

---

❤ PANDA EXPRESS

Description: Fast Chinese food

Dining Type: Quick Service

Location: Near Transformers: The Ride

Pricing: $$

Menu Overview: Orange chicken, spicy chicken, chow mein, fried rice, sushi, beer, soda.

Review: This Panda Express is similar to those found across the country, but also offers sushi. Many of these plates feature the popular orange chicken with another side. Seating is available inside the restaurant.

Recommendation: Orange Chicken with a mix of fried rice and chow mein

---

❤ STUDIO CAFE Ω

Description: Grab-and-go sandwiches

Dining Type: Quick Service

Location: Near Universal Plaza (central hub)

Pricing: $-$$

Menu Overview: Salads, hot dogs, sushi, sandwiches, chicken, desserts, tea, coffee, beer, wine.

Review: The Studio Cafe serves quick food for those on the go. The quality is usually better here, as the deli sandwiches are kept fresh all day. With a wide variety of plant-based items, this location is also great for vegans.

Recommendation: Turkey and Swiss Croissant or Vegan Quinoa Salad

MORE EATS

❤ **ISLA NUBAR** ($-$$) – Try a specialty cocktail or mixed drink at this Jurassic World-themed bar. Many of the drinks come with a souvenir cup or upgrade for a couple of bucks to a plastic tiki cup. Don't forget to tip your bartender!

❤ **STARBUCKS** ($) – Enjoy a drink or a snack from the popular coffee chain.

STUDIO SCOOP ($) – Cups of ice cream or milkshakes with swirls of whipped cream, syrup, and candy toppings. We recommend the s'mores milkshake!

❤ **SUPER SNACKS** ($) – Enjoy cream sodas and popcorn themed after Super Mario characters. This is located outside of Super Nintendo World and there are delicious peach, strawberry, and green apple cream sodas!

MUMMY EATS ($-$$) – Try a corn dog or fries at this snack station.

CITYWALK DINING

ANTOJITOS COCINA MEXICANA

Mexican dining experience with lively music

Dining Type: Table Service

Pricing: $$-$$$

Open: Lunch and Dinner

Menu Overview: Tacos, burritos, fajitas, quesadillas, nachos, soda, beer, margaritas, cocktails.

Review: Antojitos has a fun south-of-the-border ambiance with colorful décor, friendly staff, and mariachi music playing around the restaurant. While the food doesn't compare to smaller, local Mexican restaurants, it's still pretty good!

Recommendation: Chimichanga or fajitas. Their margaritas are delicious, too!

❤ BUBBA GUMP SHRIMP CO.

Forrest Gump-themed dining with plenty of shrimp and American favorites

Dining Type: Table Service

Pricing: $$-$$$

Open: Lunch and Dinner

Menu Overview: Burger, shrimp, salad, clam chowder, sandwiches, fried chicken, cocktails, beer, wine, soda.

Review: The restaurant from *Forrest Gump* comes to life with some very delicious food! Bubba Gump's has fun waiters, themed rooms from the movie, and unforgettable food. If you're a fan of fried shrimp, we highly recommend this place. However, the fried chicken is especially good, too. Before you order, your waiter asks *Forrest Gump* trivia—it's a lot of fun, even if you haven't seen the movie in years. As far as chain restaurants go, Bubba Gump wins the prize for overall customer satisfaction from us.

Recommendation: Shrimpers Heaven or Mama's Southern Fried Chicken

· **Magic Tips** ·

Landry's Select Club members get priority seating at Bubba Gump's. If you have the membership, tell the hostess before grabbing your table and you may skip wait times on busier days. To sign up for Landry's

Select Club, visit: **www.landrysselect.com**. Terms are always subject to change and you may have to pay for a small sign-up fee. However, sign-up fees usually come with a dining credit for the same amount.

BUCA DI BEPPO

Italian cuisine

Dining Type: Table Service

Pricing: $$$

Open: Lunch and Dinner

Menu Overview: Pasta, chicken, pizza, salads, desserts, soda, wine, beer.

Review: Dine on Italian-American favorites like pasta and pizza in this family-friendly chain restaurant.

Recommendation: Lasagna or Eggplant Parmigiana

DONGPO KITCHEN

Trendy Asian cuisine

Dining Type: Table Service

Pricing: $$-$$$

Open: Lunch and Dinner

Menu Overview: Chicken entrees, vegetable entrees, dumplings, potstickers, noodles, rice, soups, dessert, milk tea, soda, beer, wine.

Review: We enjoy the vibe of DongPo, and that the restaurant focuses on organic entrees. However, the food doesn't leave much of an impression. Still, it could satisfy your craving for dumplings or a noodle bowl.

Recommendation: Dan Dan Noodles

❤ JIMMY BUFFET'S MARGARITAVILLE

Island-inspired cuisine and American favorites set in a tropical atmosphere.

Dining Type: Table Service

Pricing: $$-$$$

Open: Lunch and Dinner (may stay open later on weekends)

Menu Overview: Burgers, sandwiches, tacos, shrimp, fish, kabobs, barbecue ribs, soda, margaritas, cocktails, beer.

Review: This chain restaurant is a fun escape into a tropical paradise. There's a definite "tourist attraction" feel about Margaritaville, but the lively music and delicious food are fun nonetheless.

Recommendation: Cheddar BBQ Burger or Fish Tacos. The margaritas are delicious, too!

JOHNNY ROCKETS

American diner

Dining Type: Table Service

Pricing: $$

Open: Lunch and Dinner

Menu Overview: Burgers, sandwiches, fries, shakes, soda, beer.

Review: Grab your choice of burger and shake in this classic American diner.

Recommendation: Smokehouse Burger

NBC SPORTS GRILL & BREW

Sports Bar and Grill

Dining Type: Table Service

Pricing: $$-$$$

Open: Lunch and Dinner

Menu Overview: Burgers, salads, chicken, ribs, macaroni and cheese, corn bread, fries, salmon, beer, cocktails

Review: A lively sports bar with full restaurant

Recommendation: Gruyère Burger

❤ TOOTHSOME CHOCOLATE EMPORIUM

Sweets and dishes in a steampunk themed restaurant.

Dining Type: Table service and dessert bar

Open: Lunch and Dinner (also serves Brunch all day)

Price: $$–$$$

Menu Overview: Flatbreads, salads, soups, sandwiches, hamburgers, pasta, chicken, steak, crepes, quiche, waffles, French toast, milkshakes, desserts, beer, full bar, cocktails, wine, soda

Review: The theme is like Charlie and the Chocolate Factory meets 19th century steampunk. The decor is stunning and the food looks mouthwatering. For mechanical gears to wild costumes, there's plenty to see around the room while you wait for a seat. We love looking at the array of desserts like fancy chocolates. Once seated, you'll have to resist ordering a little bit of everything. Since Toothsome's best designs are sweets, we recommend focusing more on the desserts rather than the savory entrees.

Recommendation: Come for the desserts & milkshakes

VIVO ITALIAN KITCHEN

Trendy Italian table service

Dining Type: Table Service

Pricing: $$-$$$

Open: Lunch and Dinner

Menu Overview: Pizza, pasta, salad, bolognese, lasagna, fish, chicken, lamb, wine, beer, specialty drinks, soda.

Review: In contrast with Buca di Beppo, Vivo Italian Kitchen has a more stylish vibe. Think of this as a trendy Italian restaurant with fresh takes on Italian favorites. Many of the entrees here are vegetarian.

Recommendation: The Bolognese

> · **Magic Tips** ·
> Looking for dining recommendations for kids? We list the best options for kids in the next chapter.

WASABI

Sushi Bar

Dining Type: Table Service

Pricing: $$-$$$

Open: Lunch and Dinner

Menu Overview: Sushi, tempura, chicken, soda, sake, Japanese beer, wine, cocktails.

Review: A sushi bar known for its sashimi and tempura rolls.

Recommendation: Your choice of sushi roll and a side of Shrimp and Vegetable Tempura

OTHER EATS

CHICK CHICK CHICKEN ($) – Hand-breaded chicken and chicken sandwiches

❤ **THE CREPE CAFE** ($) – Stop in for a freshly made sweet or savory breakfast crêpe. We recommend a fruit crêpe with Nutella spread!

THE HABIT BURGER ($) – Southern Californian fast food burgers, fries, and salads. We recommend the Santa Barbara Char (double burger served with cheese and avocado in a sourdough bun) with a side of onion rings!

❤ **FIREHOUSE SUBS** ($) – Signature hot and cold sandwiches.

KFC EXPRESS/PIZZA HUT EXPRESS ($) – Quick order fried chicken or personal pizzas.

❤ **PANDA EXPRESS** ($) – Fast Chinese food known for their famous orange chicken recipe.

PINK'S FAMOUS HOT DOGS ($) – Classic Los Angeles hot dogs with French fries and onion rings. May stay open later on the weekends.

TACO BELL ($) – Fast Mexican food.

SNACK SPOTS

BEN & JERRY'S ($) – A colorful store with a wide variety of delicious ice cream flavors.

CINNABON ($) – Freshly made cinnamon rolls.

JAMBA ($) – Blended fruit smoothies and snacks. A perfect stop for a quick breakfast!

MENCHIES ($) – Frozen yogurt creations with your choice of flavors and toppings.

❤ **MINI MONSTER** ($) – Boba milk teas served in cute, monster-shaped bottles.

❤ **POPCORNOPOLIS** ($) – Choose from a wide variety of sweet popcorn flavors and made-to-go desserts.

SPARKY'S MINI DONUTS AND CHOCOLATES ($) – Hot-to-order mini donuts and delicious gifts.

STARBUCKS ($) – Famous brewed coffee and pastries. Universal Studios also has two other locations within the theme park.

❤ **VOODOO DOUGHNUT** ($) – Delicious gourmet donuts in a wide variety of flavors and themes. The line can become pretty long at Voodoo Doughnuts, but it tends to die down in the late afternoon.

WETZEL'S PRETZELS ($) – Soft pretzel snacks and sodas.

SPECIAL DIETS

Though people typically associate theme park food with hot dogs and hamburgers, that's simply not the case at Universal Studios Hollywood. The theme park recognizes that its guests have a wide variety of special dietary needs and desires. Vegan and vegetarian options are available at many of the dining spots. For many entrees, Universal has options for a plant-based substitute. Always carefully review the menu or ask the counter service cashier as these options may change.

If you have a food allergy or other dietary need, please inform your server. Often, they will ask if anyone at the table has a food allergy before taking orders. However, not all dietary requests can be met. For example, the corn dog batter may not be changed, as well as the churro mix.

PACKING YOUR OWN FOOD

Guests may bring their own snacks into the theme park with some exceptions. Permitted items include things like protein bars, small bags of chips, and bottles of water 2 liters or smaller. Basically, most easy-to-carry snacks.

If you have special dietary needs, you may bring a packed meal. However, coolers and bags larger than 8.5" wide x 6" high x 6" deep are not allowed.

PROHIBITED ITEMS

Universal Studios Hollywood does not allow guests to bring their own alcohol into the park. Furthermore, guests may not consume or bring marijuana into the theme parks for any reason.

CHAPTER NINE

VISITING WITH KIDS

INTRODUCTION

Unfortunately, Universal Studios Hollywood doesn't have many attractions specifically tailored to young kids. However, that doesn't mean they can't enjoy a day in the park. With rides like Despicable Me: Minion Mayhem and the new Secret Life of Pets: Off the Leash, families with young children are finding many more options at the theme park these days.

With that said, most of the attractions for kids are in the Upper Lot. The Illuminations area near the entrance houses play areas and rides designed with kids in mind. The Wizarding World of Harry Potter and Super Nintendo World are also designed with kids in mind.

Furthermore, Universal has a plethora of characters roaming the park from films like Trolls and Kung Fu Panda. Really, there's so much more to experience—if you know where to look! In this chapter, we explore a visit to Universal Studios Hollywood when bringing kids from infants to age 9.

MEETING CHARACTERS

Universal has a surprising amount of costumed characters roaming its parks. Several franchises, including Despicable Me, Transformers, and The Simpsons, have special character meets designed with the entire family in mind.

On busier days, some characters can have 30-minute waits. However, on less crowded days, some of the characters roam the Upper Lot greeting guests. The morning is a fantastic time to see many popular characters waiving at guests as they arrive in the parks. You can also stop and snap a photo with them against scenic backdrops!

· **Magic Tips** ·
For character appearance times, visit the official site: **USHWaitTimes.com**. Keep in mind that not all characters appear each day.

CHARACTER ENCOUNTERS

THE MINIONS

Location: Upper Lot

See the Minions from *Despicable Me* in Super Silly Fun Land in the Upper Lot. At times, several Minions roam the area, interacting with families and posing for photos.

DREAMWORKS CHARACTERS

Location: Upper Lot

Characters from *Trolls*, *Shrek*, *Madagascar*, and *Kung Fu Panda* greet guests near the Dreamworks Theatre in the Upper Lot. You may even meet all of them at once!

THE SIMPSONS

Location: Upper Lot

Homer, Bart, Marge, Lisa, and Maggie pose with guests near the Kwik-E-Mart in Springfield, U.S.A. Krusty the Clown and Sideshow Bob also make appearances.

TRANSFORMERS

Location: Lower Lot

Meet a giant Optimus Prime, Bumblebee, and even Megatron just outside of the ride in the Lower Lot. The Transformer character encounters are some of the best as they perfectly interact with guests. If meeting characters is a priority, we recommend heading to this one early in the day.

JURASSIC WORLD DINOSAURS

Location: Lower Lot

Blue the Velociraptor, Juliet the Triceratops, and even some baby dinos greet guests near Jurassic World – The Ride. Blue may be a bit scary for kids under 8, but Juliet is slow-moving and very friendly. Baby dinos may only appear seasonally.

SUPER MARIO CHARACTERS

Location: Lower Lot

Meet Mario, Luigi, Princess Peach, and Toad in Nintendo World! The Power-Up Bands also allow kids to interact with the land.

MORE CHARACTERS

Dora the Explorer (Upper Lot)

Curious George (Upper Lot)

Hello Kitty (Upper Lot, near the Animation Studio Store)

Scooby Doo & Shaggy (Upper Lot)

SpongeBob & Patrick (Upper Lot near Universal Plaza)

CHILD SWITCH

The rides at Universal offer a "Child Switch" feature for families with children too short (or too scared) to ride. Child Switch works by allowing one adult to wait while the other rides. When the second adult returns, they "switch" and the first adult experiences the attraction while the other waits with the child. This way, parents and older kids can ride without losing their place in line to wait with a younger child.

To use Child Switch, you'll need to inform a team member at the entrance to the attraction. From there, you'll be instructed to either wait in a special room before switching or experience a play area like Super Silly Fun Land. Some of the waiting areas play movies or have activities for young kids to enjoy while they wait.

BABIES AND TODDLERS

Unlike Disney theme parks, Universal Studios Hollywood doesn't have a designated child care center. Instead, it offers changing tables in all restrooms and a nursing spot in the First Aid Station.

FIRST AID LOCATIONS

Upper Lot – Next to French Street Bistro
Lower Lot – Next to Jurassic World – The Ride

STROLLERS

Universal encourages its guests to bring single or double strollers into the parks. If you need to rent one, they are available just past the entrance to the park. Single strollers are $15 a day and doubles are $25.

BABIES & TODDLERS TIPS

When bringing a young child to a theme park, we always recommend taking your time. If possible, knock out the "must-do" rides and attractions within the first 3-4 hours. After that, we recommend taking a break for an hour or two before returning. Getting a reservation at CityWalk or taking a break at your hotel are great ways to recharge.

While there aren't many rides designed for babies and toddlers at Universal, we've listed some experiences they might enjoy:

Super Silly Fun Land (Upper Lot) – An outdoor water playground inspired by *Despicable Me*. Kids must be 48" or smaller to play. Note that this attraction area could be closed during the off season and some weekdays.

Silly Swirly Fun Ride (Upper Lot) – Perhaps the only ride suitable for babies and toddlers, this spinner attraction is similar to Dumbo the Flying Elephant at Disneyland.

DreamWorks Theatre Featuring Kung Foo Panda (Upper Lot) – A giant, immersive theater with moving seats. Young kids who need to sit on a parent's lap must use non-moving seats. This show may be too loud for some young kids.

Secret Life of Pets (Upper Lot) – Kids 34" (87cm) or taller can enjoy this colorful and funny ride based on *The Secret Life of Pets* films.

Despicable Me: Minion Mayhem (Upper Lot) – Designed for kids 40" (102cm), this action-filled attraction is great for the entire family.

⋆ Magic Tips ⋆
The World-Famous Studio Tour doesn't have a minimum height requirement, however, it's too scary for most young kids. The entire experience is 60 minutes and has some frightening action sequences include an attacking shark from *Jaws* and a gruesome battle with King Kong.

If you still want to bring your young child, place them in the center of the tram. Their view will be limited and help reduce some of their fright.

KIDS (AGES 4-9)

The fun of Universal Studios Hollywood mostly relies on the visitor's thrill level. For example, even if your child is tall enough to ride Harry Potter and the Forbidden Journey, they still might not enjoy it. The attraction contains the magic and scary creatures from the Harry Potter films and some kids find this too scary. To better help decide which attractions are best for your child, we've made a list of scare levels.

RIDE SCARE LEVELS

HIGH THRILL (SCARY)
- Jurassic World – The Ride
- Revenge of the Mummy

MEDIUM THRILL (SOME SCARES)
- Harry Potter and the Forbidden Journey
- Transformers: The Ride 3D

- World-Famous Studio Tour

LITTLE THRILL (EXCITING SEQUENCES, NO SCARE)

- Despicable Me: Minion Mayhem
- DreamWorks Theatre Featuring Kung Fu Panda
- Flight of the Hippogriff (roller coaster)
- The Secret Life of Pets: Off the Leash
- The Simpsons Ride
- WaterWorld

NO THRILL (NOT SCARY)

- DinoPlay (playground near Jurassic World)
- Super Silly Fun Land

BEST DINING FOR KIDS

As far as kid-friendliness goes, not all restaurants are created equal. We've stopped at all locations around Universal Studios Hollywood and found the best dining for kids. These are quick-service and table service eateries with better menu options designed for kids under 10.

UNIVERSAL STUDIOS HOLLYWOOD - UPPER LOT

- Three Broomsticks – *Top Choice!*
- Luigi's Pizza
- Cletus' Chicken Shack

UNIVERSAL STUDIOS HOLLYWOOD - LOWER LOT

- Jurassic Cafe – *Top Choice!*
- Panda Express
- Mummy Eats

UNIVERSAL CITYWALK

- Bubba Gump Shrimp Co. – *Top Choice!*
- Johnny Rockets
- Blaze Pizza

CHAPTER TEN

HALLOWEEN HORROR NIGHTS

INTRODUCTION

If you're a fan of Halloween, autumn might be your favorite time to visit Universal Studios Hollywood! Every year, the theme park throws a scare-tastic bash known as Halloween Horror Nights. This epic, park-wide event is filled with haunted mazes, Scare Zones, creepy treats, spooky stage shows—and so much more! Mostly popular with adults, the park transforms at sundown into a terrifying and ghastly world. You'll see your favorite horror movies and scary TV series come to life in this unique experience.

Halloween Horror Nights (HHN) is a separate ticketed nighttime event that takes place in September and October (and sometimes the first few days of November). While most of the rides are open, the haunted mazes are the best part. Starting at the entrance, creepy demons and "serial killers" roam foggy streets. Each year holds a new set of terrifying surprises.

WHEN IS HHN?

The event takes place from mid-September through the first week of November. Tickets usually go on sale during the summer and sell out by mid-September.

WHAT ARE THE SCARE ZONES AND MAZES?
Scare Zones and Mazes are frightening areas where horror franchises come to life. You might be chased by a chainsaw-wielding Jason or escape the wrath of killers from *The Purge* series. *American Horror Story, Nightmare on Elm Street, The Walking Dead, The Shining*, and *Saw* have all made appearances at HHN. Universal usually begins announcing maze and Scare Zone themes in the summer before the event.

· Magic Tips ·
Some attractions may get Halloween overlays for the event. In the past, Jurassic Park (which is now Jurassic World) and the Studio Tour have added features to make the night even more frightening.

SHOULD I BRING MY CHILD?
Probably not. Even if your kid can handle watching a horror movie, they'll likely feel frightened when a gang of nightmarish creatures chases them down the street. We sometimes do see kids at HHN, and we've also seen many of them crying their eyes out. The scare actors do not go easy on them. The general consensus is that the event is for teens and older. So, wait until your child turns 13 and you can reexamine if they are ready.

PURCHASING DISCOUNTED TICKETS
Buy early! Universal announces Halloween Horror Nights usually six months before the event. Tickets usually go on sale in the summer and prices increase in the weeks leading up to the event. Also, popular dates sell out quickly (like weekends and Halloween night). The least-expensive tickets are in September through the first week of October. Weekdays are also cheaper (though HHN isn't open on every weeknight).

Universal will often hold a promotion with Coca-Cola or other popular brands for discounted tickets on select dates. Furthermore, annual passholders get a discounted or free ticket, depending on their pass type. These discounts are usually listed before purchasing tickets: www.HalloweenHorrorNights.com.

Note: We have seen many people get turned away from the event or purchase the wrong Halloween Horror Night tickets. When visiting the website, make sure that you are purchasing tickets for Hollywood and not Orlando.

PREPARING FOR LONG LINES

Since most of the dates sell out for Halloween Horror Nights, the lines become incredibly long. In the past, some of the popular mazes have had 5-hour wait times! For this reason, we recommend visiting in September and arriving early.

EXPRESS PASS

You can also purchase an Express Pass (usually around $100 or more in addition to the theme park ticket) to skip the lines and complete all the mazes. You likely won't get to experience every maze in a single night without Express Pass. Every year, there are very popular mazes that have the longest lines. Keep in mind, the daytime Express Pass will not work for HHN.

· Magic Tips ·

Universal sells Express Passes that work after 10PM for about half of the normal cost. To save money and time, we recommend buying one of these at the start of your night as they tend to sell out before 10PM. Look for an Express Pass distribution kiosk.

CHAPTER ELEVEN

HOTELS & OTHER DESTINATIONS

INTRODUCTION

From our experience, theme parks are generally categorized into two different types: resorts and parks. Theme park resorts typically have hotel accommodations directly on-site. Universal Orlando, for instance, has several hotels surrounding its theme parks for guests to stay during their visit. Additionally, these hotel guests receive special benefits like early theme park entrance.

However, Universal Studios Hollywood only fits into the "park" category. Even though Universal Hollywood sometimes partners with nearby Los Angeles hotels, guests stay off property and don't receive amenities like in Orlando.

Furthermore, Los Angeles is the second-most populated city in the United States. LA stretches over 460 square miles and is home to more than 1,000 hotels.

Since we can't categorize and rank every Los Angeles hotel in one theme park guide, we've decided to narrow it down to our top picks. These are chain and boutique establishments located near the theme park. Since we're focused on positive reviews, we've intentionally left out hotels that we don't recommend.

CLOSEST HOTELS

HILTON UNIVERSAL CITY

555 Universal Hollywood Dr, Universal City, CA 91608
(818) 506-2500 / www.hilton.com

Distance from Universal: About 0.5 miles
Cost: Moderate **Star Rating:** 4
Review: The Hilton Universal City is just a 5-10 minute walk to the gate of Universal Studios Hollywood. Free shuttle service is also available. This clean, well-run hotel is home to Cafe Sierra, a restaurant within a stylish glass atrium. Dining is provided here all day, including an American breakfast, lunch, and dinner. Garaged guest parking is $30/night.
Amenities: Outdoor Pool with Hot Tub • Free WiFi • Fitness Center • Restaurant • Optional Pet Rooms
Discounts: Hilton offers discounts for AAA, AARP, seniors, and government employees directly through their website.

SHERATON UNIVERSAL HOTEL

333 Universal Hollywood Dr, Universal City, CA 91608
(818) 980-1212 / www.sheraton.com

Distance from Universal: About 4 miles
Cost: Moderate **Star Rating:** 4
Review: The Sheraton Universal hotel tower is easily seen from the theme park entrance and is a 5-10 minute walk to Universal Studios. Sheraton is part of the Marriott hotel family and is widely known for quality, moderately-priced hotel rooms. However, guests can see sweeping views of Los Angeles when booking a room on a higher floor. While the Sheraton excels in location and cleanliness, the service level at this hotel may feel underwhelming when considering the price. Pricing for Sheraton Universal fluctuates depending on

seasonal crowds. Guests must pay for their own parking at $38/night.

Amenities: Outdoor Pool with Hot Tub • Free WiFi • Fitness Center • Restaurants • Optional Pet Rooms

Discounts: Book early or use AAA to get a discount when you reserve a room directly through Sheraton.com.

TOP BUDGET-FRIENDLY HOTELS

BLVD HOTEL & SPA

10730 Ventura Blvd, Studio City, CA 91604

(818) 623-9100 / www.blvdstudiocity.com

Star Rating	Our Rating	Price	Free Parking	Pool
3	B+	Value	No	Yes

A boutique hotel within a 10-minute walk to Universal Studios Hollywood. Guests can also walk to the LA Metro Station in just 5 minutes! Rooms here have vivid, swanky decor and offer family-friendly accommodations.

The BLVD Hotel is also home to an indoor pool, fitness room, cafe, and lounge. The spa has massage treatments; booking ahead is recommended: (818) 623-9100. Guests also have access to free WiFi.

Overall, we recommend the BLVD Hotel for location, price, and amenities. Keep in mind that garage parking here is $31/night.

THE TANGERINE

3901 Riverside Drive, Burbank, CA 91505

(818) 843-1121 / www.thetangerine.com

Star Rating	Our Rating	Price	Free Parking	Pool
2	A	Value	Yes	Yes

The Tangerine lives up to its name with orange hues around the property. From carrot-colored stairs to apricot-shaded pillows, this hotel's retro feel is everywhere. While The Tangerine only has very basic rooms, it's about a 5-minute drive to Universal Studios Hollywood.

Guests are treated to free parking, free WiFi, and a delicious complimentary breakfast with their stay. While you might save on nightly costs at another hotel, the free parking and breakfast more than make up for it. Breakfast is provided daily from 7 AM until 11 AM (Sundays are 7:30 AM - 11 AM).

THE GARLAND

4222 Vineland Ave, North Hollywood, CA 91602
(818) 980-8000 / www.thegarland.com

Star Rating	Our Rating	Price	Free Parking	Pool
3	A	Moderate	No	Yes

Many Hollywood boutique hotels around enjoy keeping a swanky, mid-century vibe—and The Garland is no exception. Located near Universal City, this hotel has an outdoor pool and restaurant, The Front Yard. This outdoor dining experience has a full bar and serves delicious breakfast, lunch, and dinner for its guests.

Overall, The Garland has friendly staff, clean rooms, and a central location. Guests can also take a free shuttle from the hotel to Universal Studios Hollywood. The shuttle runs almost every hour and drops guests off at CityWalk. WiFi at The Garland is complimentary, but self-parking is $29/night.

BEST WESTERN PLUS MEDIA CENTER INN & SUITES

3910 W Riverside Dr, Burbank, CA 91505
(818) 842-1900 / www.bestwestern.com

Star Rating	Our Rating	Price	Free Parking	Pool
3	B+	Value	No	Yes

The Best Western Plus Media Center is another great choice for its free parking, free breakfast, and central location. Guests also have access to complimentary WiFi.

While this Best Western doesn't have shuttle service to Universal Studios Hollywood, it is only about a 10-minute drive to the theme park.

HOMESTAY OPTIONS

In recent years, homestay options like Airbnb have become increasingly popular. Using a website, guests can book a room or entire home during their stay. These aren't hotel rooms, but private homes owned and operated by everyday people.

For many travelers, using one of these services is the most affordable way to stay in Los Angeles. Renting a home can be a fraction of the cost of hotels. While you may miss out on many of the luxuries of a hotel, some homes are beautiful, very central, and often offer free parking.

Keep in mind that Los Angeles is a city where cars are all but mandatory. No matter where you'll stay, be sure to budget for a rental car or rideshare service like Lyft.

To use Airbnb, visit their website at airbnb.com or download the mobile app. We recommend browsing their site and reading user reviews before booking.

OTHER DESTINATIONS

If you're planning an extended stay in Los Angeles, Southern California is filled with world-class sights and amusements to make your trip even more memorable! Universal Studios Hollywood is just a few minutes away from iconic Los Angeles attractions and about 35 miles (56 km) from Disneyland. Meaning, you could plan a single day trip to several Hollywood sites or even Disneyland with ease. Here, we've outlined tips and travel advice for visiting the sites beyond Universal Studios.

LOS ANGELES

HOLLYWOOD

Visit the Hollywood Walk of Fame, the famous Grauman's Chinese Theatre, and the Hollywood Highland Center where the Academy Awards are filmed. On the way, you'll see the Hollywood Sign high up on the hills. We will warn you that while Hollywood is a cool sight-seeing and photo-op place, it's not the fanciest. It's an authentic downtown location and the streets can feel dirty. For something posher, shop on Rodeo Drive or head to West Hollywood nearby.

· **Magic Tips** ·

The iconic Hollywood sign can easily be seen from around town or by car off the 101 freeway. However, the best way to see this landmark is from Griffith Park (*2800 East Observatory Road, Los Angeles, CA 90027*). Parking is $8-$10/hour.

GETTY CENTER

1200 Getty Center Dr, Los Angeles, CA 90049

See an exquisite art museum in a state-of-the-art building near Hollywood. There's also a tram that transports you to the museum! Admission is free, but parking is $20.

WARNER BROS. STUDIO TOUR

3400 Warner Blvd, Burbank, CA 91522

Take a behind-the-scenes tour of Warner Bros. Studio!s Located just a couple miles from Universal Studios Hollywood, this tour gives guests a sneak peek of sets from *Friends*, *Gilmore Girls*, *Wonder Woman*, and more! However, the 3-hour tour changes frequently depending on whether a soundstage is being used for filming.

Guests must be at least 8 years old and much of the tour is on foot. Photography and video may also be limited during many experiences. Tickets start at $69 per adult ($59 for kids 8-12) when purchased in advance.
Booking: www.wbstudiotour.com

DISNEYLAND

DISNEYLAND RESORT

1313 South Harbor Blvd, Anaheim, CA 92802

The celebrated theme park that started it all is located just 30-40 minutes by car from Universal Studios Hollywood. Split into two theme parks—Disneyland and Disney California Adventure—the Disneyland Resort is filled with both kid-friendly and thrilling attractions. The original park is home to Mickey and Minnie Mouse, Disney Princesses, and the all-new Star Wars: Galaxy's Edge. Disney California Adventure, located within walking distance from Disneyland, houses several attractions based on Pixar and Marvel characters.

Tickets for a single park start at $104 per guest, but prices change depending on the day. All-day parking is available for $30. We offer a full guide to the Disneyland Resort that details planning, the best restaurants, and how to save money during your stay. For more information, visit: www.magicguidebooks.com/books.

CHAPTER TWELVE

BEST-OF LISTS

OUR LISTS

When planning your trip, you may feel that there are far too many options. Though we do our best to condense the information in this guide, we recognize that it can still feel fairly stuffed. To help sort these options, we've compiled valuable lists with our most recommended experiences. In this chapter, we highlight the best that Universal Studios Hollywood has to offer!

> **Note:** This list does not include attractions found in Super Nintendo World.

We've compiled this list in order with 1 being the most recommended:

BEST THRILL RIDES

1. Harry Potter and the Forbidden Journey
2. Jurassic World – The Ride
3. Transformers: The Ride 3D
4. Revenge of the Mummy
5. The World-Famous Studio Tour

BEST FAMILY RIDES

1. The World-Famous Studio Tour
2. The Secret Life of Pets: Off the Leash!
3. Transformers: The Ride 3D
4. Despicable Me: Minion Mayhem
5. DreamWorks Theatre: Kung Fu Panda

BEST NON-RIDE ATTRACTIONS

1. Exploring Hogsmeade Village
2. WaterWorld
3. Ollivanders
4. DreamWorks Theatre: Kung Fu Panda (stationary seats)

BEST SNACKS

1. Butterbeer (Butterbeer Cart in Hogsmeade Village)
2. The Big Pink (Lard Lad Donuts, Upper Lot)
3. ? Block Tiramisu (Toadstool Cafe, Lower Lot)
4. Princess Peach's Peach Soda (Super Snacks, Lower Lot)
5. Churros (various carts around the park)

BEST QUICK-SERVICE RESTAURANTS

1. Three Broomsticks (Hogsmeade Village)
2. Jurassic Cafe (Lower Lot)
3. Bumblebee Man's Tacos (Upper Lot)
4. Cletus' Chicken Shack (Upper Lot)
5. The Crepe Cafe (CityWalk)

BEST CITYWALK RESTAURANTS

1. Jimmy Buffet's Margaritaville
2. Samba Brazilian Steakhouse
3. Bubba Gump Shrimp Co.
4. Karl Strauss Brewing Company
5. Antojitos Cocina Mexican

CHAPTER THIRTEEN

PRE-PLANNED ATTRACTION LISTS

INTRODUCTION

Many travelers who visit Universal Studios Hollywood are worried about not experiencing everything they want to during their stay. With so many choices, it might be impossible to get everything done in one day without a plan. However, with our pre-made ride and attraction lists, you can enjoy the very best that Universal has to offer. These are *proven* to work using multiple tests over several visits. Thus, we recommend following one of our pre-made guides in order to accomplish the most on a busy day—even if you don't purchase Express Pass!

TIME-SAVING TIPS:

1. Download the Universal Studios Hollywood mobile app before you arrive to the park.
2. Get to the park early and grab a map at the entrance.
3. Take a photo of the ride list you've chosen with your phone or cut it out to take with you.
4. Reserve all table-service dining before arrival.
5. Take a break when you need to in between rides.
6. Keep calm, enjoy the sights, and have fun!

MUST-SEE ATTRACTIONS PLAN

1. **Mario Kart: Bowser's Challenge** (Lower Lot)
   May need to join Virtual Line *
2. **Jurassic World—The Ride** (Lower Lot)
3. **Revenge of the Mummy** (Lower Lot)
4. **Transformers: The Ride 3D** (Lower Lot)
5. **Explore Super Nintendo World** (Lower Lot) **
6. **The Simpsons Ride** (Upper Lot)
7. **The World-Famous Studio Tour** (Upper Lot)
8. **The Secret Life of Pets: Off the Leash*** (Upper Lot)
9. **Despicable Me: Minion Mayhem** (Upper Lot)
10. **WaterWorld** (Upper Lot)
11. **Ollivanders** (Upper Lot)
12. **Harry Potter and the Forbidden Journey** (Upper Lot)
13. **Flight of the Hippogriff** (Upper Lot)
14. **Explore Hogsmeade Village** (Upper Lot)
15. **DreamWorks Theatre: Kung Fu Panda** (Upper Lot)

* May need to use the Universal Studios Hollywood mobile app to access the Virtual Line.

Note: Super Nintendo World may require guests to access the land using the Virtual Line. In this instance, you would want to explore Super Nintendo World right after riding the Mario Kart attraction. Then, go onto Jurassic World and other rides in this list.

If there is not a virtual queue or wait for the land, follow in the above order.

WITH KIDS AGES 3-5 PLAN

1. **Mario Kart: Bowser's Challenge** (Lower Lot)
   May need to join Virtual Line *
2. **Explore Super Nintendo World** (Lower Lot)
3. **The Secret Life of Pets: Off the Leash** (Upper Lot)
4. **Despicable Me: Minion Mayhem** (Upper Lot)
5. **Explore Hogsmeade Village** (Upper Lot)
6. **Ollivanders** (Upper Lot)
7. **Silly Swirly Fun Ride** (Upper Lot)
8. **Super Silly Fun Land** (Upper Lot) **
9. **DreamWorks Theatre: Kung Fu Panda** (Upper Lot)

* May need to use the Universal Studios Hollywood mobile app to access the Virtual Line. Check height requirements for Mario Kart before entering the queue.

** Seasonal attraction. Kids will get wet! If this play area isn't open, try DinoPlay in the Lower Lot near Jurassic World—The Ride.

WITH KIDS AGES 6-9 PLAN

1. **Mario Kart: Bowser's Challenge** (Lower Lot)
   May need to join Virtual Line *
2. **Explore Super Nintendo World** (Lower Lot)
3. **Transformers: The Ride 3D** (Lower Lot)
4. **Harry Potter and the Forbidden Journey** (Upper Lot) **
5. **Flight of the Hippogriff** (Upper Lot)
6. **The Simpsons Ride** (Upper Lot)
7. *Join the virtual queue for The Secret Life of Pets*
8. **The World-Famous Studio Tour** (Upper Lot)
9. **The Secret Life of Pets: Off the Leash** (Upper Lot)
10. **Despicable Me: Minion Mayhem** (Upper Lot)
11. **Super Silly Fun Land** (Upper Lot) ***
12. **WaterWorld** (Upper Lot)
13. **Ollivanders** (Upper Lot)
14. **Explore Hogsmeade Village** (Upper Lot)
15. **DreamWorks Theatre: Kung Fu Panda** (Upper Lot)

* May need to use the Universal Studios Hollywood mobile app to access the Virtual Line.

** Attraction may be too scary for kids in this age range.

*** Seasonal attraction. Kids will get wet! If this play area isn't open, try DinoPlay in the Lower Lot near Jurassic World—The Ride.

CUSTOM RIDE LIST

1. ______________________________
2. ______________________________
3. ______________________________
4. ______________________________
5. ______________________________
6. ______________________________
7. ______________________________
8. ______________________________
9. ______________________________
10. ______________________________
11. ______________________________
12. ______________________________
13. ______________________________
14. ______________________________
15. ______________________________
16. ______________________________
17. ______________________________
18. ______________________________
19. ______________________________
20. ______________________________

CUSTOM RIDE LIST

1. ______________________________
2. ______________________________
3. ______________________________
4. ______________________________
5. ______________________________
6. ______________________________
7. ______________________________
8. ______________________________
9. ______________________________
10. ______________________________
11. ______________________________
12. ______________________________
13. ______________________________
14. ______________________________
15. ______________________________
16. ______________________________
17. ______________________________
18. ______________________________
19. ______________________________
20. ______________________________

GUESTS WITH DISABILITIES

Universal Studios accommodates guests with disabilities in a few ways. While these programs help, they aren't perfect. Unfortunately, not all rides can accommodate every person's needs, so adjustments to your plans may be needed.

MOBILITY

Guests with mobility challenges may want to bring their own wheelchair or Electronic Conveyance Vehicle (ECV). For those wishing to rent a transport, manual wheelchairs are $15 per day and ECVs are $60 at Guest Services. Wheelchairs also require a $25 deposit that is refundable upon return.

Universal Studios also provides accessible parking for those with disabilities. Parking structures and lots will have signage directing guests to these locations.

⋆ **Magic Tips** ⋆

The Universal StarWay escalators are required for visiting the Lower Lot on your own. If you are unable to take the escalator, a shuttle guides guests with disabilities down. To access these shuttles, check in with a Team Member at the top of the escalators.

ATTRACTION ASSISTANCE PASS

Universal Studios Hollywood has its own dedicated Attraction Assistance Pass simply known as AAP. Universal designed this pass for guests who cannot wait in conventional queues and lines. AAP works similarly to Express Pass, allowing guests and their traveling party to use a specified entrance that skips the line. However, you may still need to wait up to 30 minutes. If the line is too long, Universal may issue you a return time. While you wait, you can experience other attractions around the park.

Additionally, traveling parties may be limited to 4 guests per AAP. To obtain an AAP, visit Guest Relations shortly after entering the theme park. Universal will ask what type of assistance you need to determine if the AAP is right for you. Typically, they are accommodating to those with both visible and hidden disabilities. Passes expire at the end of the day.

HEARING ACCESSIBILITY

For those with difficulties hearing, Universal Studios' Guest Relations distributes Assistive Listening Systems free of charge. Select attractions and shows will work with these devices. Sign language interpreters can be requested on UniversalStudiosHollywood.com (in the contact section) or by calling (800) 864-8377 and pressing 9. Universal asks that you make your request at least one week before your arrival.

SERVICE ANIMALS

Universal Studios Hollywood welcomes guests with trained service animals. However, the guest must be in charge of their service animal at all times. Team Members are not permitted to assist with your animal regardless of the situation. Furthermore, rides don't allow for service animals. Guest Relations has an updated list of attractions that restrict service animals. Animals are permitted for potty breaks around the park, and owners must clean up afterward.

⋆ **Magic Tips** ⋆

Universal may change their disability access, so it's important that you keep up with the latest information. To read more, visit **UniversalStudiosHollywood.com**.

VACATION CHECKLIST

- ❑ Park tickets
- ❑ Ride list
- ❑ ID
- ❑ Credit card / cash
- ❑ Hotel address
- ❑ Phone (and charging cable)
- ❑ Sunscreen
- ❑ Toiletries: toothbrush, toothpaste, etc.
- ❑ Swimsuit
- ❑ Jacket
- ❑ Comfortable shoes
- ❑ Plastic bag for cellphone (water rides)
- ❑ Snacks
- ❑ Water bottles (if you aren't flying)
- ❑ Backpack or bag
- ❑ Restaurant reservations
- ❑ Universal Studios Hollywood 2024 by Magic Guidebooks
- ❑ ______________________________
- ❑ ______________________________
- ❑ ______________________________
- ❑ ______________________________
- ❑ ______________________________
- ❑ ______________________________
- ❑ ______________________________
- ❑ ______________________________
- ❑ ______________________________
- ❑ ______________________________

CONCLUSION

Universal Studios Hollywood is always changing and so will this guide throughout the years. This is our third version in the series and we want to thank you for supporting us! We sincerely hope that this book is a valuable resource for you.

Although Universal Studios Hollywood is centrally located in Los Angeles, this spot also has restrictions. Because Universal only has so much land, they often must replace old attractions with newer ones. For example, The Simpsons Ride was once Back to the Future: The Ride and Revenge of the Mummy was previously the E. T. Adventure.

However, Universal Destinations & Experiences, the division of NBCUniversal that runs the theme parks, is dedicated to bringing exciting experiences to its Los Angeles park. In the coming years, a new *Fast & the Furious*-themed roller coaster will thrill guests! While we await more details, we're excited to see what the future holds!

Happy and safe travels!

Magic Guidebooks

INDEX

A

B

C

D

E

F

H

J

K

L

M

N

O

P

Q

R

S

T

U

V

W

DINING

We did not index most restaurants as they are available in alphabetical order by resort area in the Dining Guide chapter.

Was this book helpful?

★★★★★

If so, can you please leave us a quick review on Amazon.com?

Your reviews GREATLY help us out!
THANK YOU!

Wishing you a magical vacation!
Magic Guidebooks

Made in the USA
Las Vegas, NV
23 November 2024

12488572R00085